Homeless

Stairwell Books

Published by Stairwell Books

70 Barbara Drive
Norwalk
CT 06851 USA

161 Lowther Street
York, YO31 7LZ

ISBN: 978-1-939269-28-7

Second Printing

Cover Art: Tina Firthlock
Layout: Alan Gillott
Printed and bound in the UK by Russell Press

Acknowledgements

Firstly, huge thanks are due to Ross Raisin for agreeing to support our competition as judge. Ross had the hardest job of all, choosing the winner and runners up from the shortlist. We also have Ross to thank for introducing us to ARVON and Penguin who both kindly supported the competition.

We would also like to thank our volunteers Morag Caunt, Jess Goodacre, Angie Huby, Andy Humphrey, Helen Hiorns, Alison Taft and Philip Tebble who took on the task of promoting the competition throughout the UK, as well as the difficult task of shortlisting. Without their help, the competition would not have attracted as many entries as it did and we would not have had their expert input in arriving at a shortlist.

We are very grateful to ARVON for generously donating the wonderful five-day residential course as our first prize and to WH Smiths and Penguin for donating our other runners-up prizes.

Of course, without all those writers who sent in their entries there would have been no competition. Our thanks to everyone who took on the challenge of writing on the theme of 'Homeless' and sent in so many diverse and compelling pieces. The fact that we were unable to shortlist to 20 as originally planned and had to include 22 in the anthology is testament to the quality of the entries received.

Last but not least, we would also like to thank Rose Drew and Alan Gillott at Stairwell books for supporting SASH to produce and publish this very important anthology. We hope that it will be read by many and provide some insight into the lives of those who find themselves, for whatever reason, homeless or at risk of homelessness.

Front cover – Pencil Drawing – *Jade* by Tina Firthlock

Proceeds from this book will be donated to SASH, 107-109 Walmgate, York, YO1 9UA. Readers are invited to make a personal donation.

SASH
Preventing
Youth
Homelessness
Together

Winners

3rd place highly commended – Carmel Page – *Two Cushions and a Pillow*

2nd place highly commended – Alison Hitchcock – *A Seat on the Bus*

Winner and 1st place is Olivia Gwyne - *Heading North*

Table of Contents

Introduction

The writers in this anthology, whose work was selected from over a hundred and twenty entries to the competition, were given one simple prompt – the title: 'Homeless'. As a result, this book is in part a reflection on what the word – and the other word within it, the one it strives toward: 'Home' – means. The myriad of style and approach to the responses is indicative of the myriad meanings that those words hold for each of us. 'Home' is never as simple as just a place in which to live, just as 'homeless' is never as simple as solely being without that.

The importance of a charity like SASH is that it deals with the whole, alongside dealing with a person's immediate need. The emergency service which SASH runs assists young people when they find themselves at a time of crisis, but just as valuable is the operation that supports long-term lodgings, and the guidance towards education, skills and independence.

The opportunity to express one's creativity is a part of expressing independence, individuality, and as such this anthology works against all of the stigma and simplification that is ingrained in the word of its title. It feels especially important, at a time when the double whammy of welfare cuts and cuts to the funding of services that would normally deal with the after effects, has created such a sharp rise in homelessness, to hear the voices of people for whom homelessness, or the risk of it, is a reality. And young people especially – as it is young people who are often the worst affected in hard times

Fiction, I believe, has the ability to show us that reality, and make us think about it, be moved by it, laugh about it. We feel the world of a story often more minutely, more deeply – more as a human – than the world that is filtered to us through the media, the internet. Which is why this anthology, as well as the other hundred or so entries, provides such a valuable record of a moment in history. And one that, I hope, will give a lot of pleasure, and thought, to anybody who reads it.

Ross Raisin

Anna Mazzola

How to be Invisible

Shall I tell you how to be invisible?

You don't need any expensive potions or complex scientific methods – no cloaks or amulets, optics or lasers. You simply sit on a pavement in a busy street, your legs crossed behind a paper cup, your expression blank, your mind empty, and you wait. That's how I'm sitting now, next to the cash machine in the train station, watching people's feet as they walk past: commuters in smart brogues and suits, students in trainers and jeans, women in sandals and long flowing skirts, all apparently oblivious to my presence. Their eyes slide sideways, or upwards. Anywhere to avoid the space where I am. When I speak, to ask for some change, my words evaporate into the air, unheard. Occasionally, someone will stop and drop a few coins into the cup, but even these people are unable to look at me. It's as though I don't exist.

I am not here.

When we were little, my brother would hide by clutching his hands over his eyes. We were generous then, my sister and me (if only we'd been as thoughtful later) and we'd pretend we couldn't find him. It's not generosity that prevents these people from seeing me now. What is it? Shame? Anger? Disinterest?

I wonder how my family are. In the five months since I left, I haven't spoken to them once. I know they must be worried, but the more time that passes, the more difficult it becomes to contact them. If I were to call now, how would I explain? What would I say? I can't tell them about the money I owe or the things I've done. I can't communicate the strange emptiness I feel. Even if I were to try, they wouldn't understand. As my mum has told me often enough, they've always managed, even during the worst of it all. '*Through thick and thin, Samantha.*' For them, giving up was never an option, so, by running away, I've failed. I imagine Dad's fury and Mum's tears on the other end of the telephone line. Or, worse, silence.

A man's feet stop beside me. Polished brown lace-up shoes and golf socks.

'It's getting late,' he says. 'Shouldn't you be going home?'

I look up towards tweedy trousers and mustard jumper. Thick glasses conceal his eyes.

'Yeah, I'll go soon,' I say.

A pause. Then, softly, 'You could come with me.'

Ah, another of them. I've never been that pretty and I'm certainly not now, but it doesn't seem to matter to his kind – the dusk prowlers. I guess it's enough that I'm young and vulnerable. I lower my head, letting my fringe fall over my face. He waits for a few seconds until he realises I'm not going to move or reply, and then leaves. Maybe he's right: maybe I should be going home. But I can't.

It was in April that I disappeared. The pink-papered walls of my childhood bedroom had begun to collapse in on me. All of the things that had been keeping me awake – the guilt, the debt, the deceit – fused into a stifling mass, and I realised I couldn't be there anymore. Taking only a small rucksack, and telling no-one where I was going, I left my parents' house, walked through the thin rain to the coach station, and used my remaining cash to buy a ticket for the next coach. That's how I ended up here, in York, with a new name and no money.

As the darkness gathers, the night creatures emerge: the lonely, the damaged, the drunk and angry. The man in the mustard jumper reappears and watches me, silently, his gaze brushing over my skin like the wings of a moth. In my paper cup, I have just enough money for a meal – even the invisible need to eat. I consider my options. You shouldn't go too regularly to the same place. Better if they don't get to know who you are; don't ask questions. This evening, I choose a faded pizza joint and sit in a plastic seat by the window as I eat. I try to take slow, even bites, but it's the first food I've tasted all day and I'm shaky with hunger. By the time I finish, the cheap melted cheese and doughy base sit heavy in my stomach, together with another cloying feeling I can't quite identify. I stay in the café for as long as I can, my hands around a Styrofoam cup of tea, thinking about the family outings we made to Pizza Hut when I was a child. My brother, Billy, would never eat the crusts or touch his bowl of salad. There was almost always an argument. (*'How will you grow up to be a man if you don't eat?' – 'Maybe I don't want to grow up.' – 'Why can't you just leave him alone?'* And so on.)

By half past ten, I'm the only remaining customer. The staff in the café start stacking the chairs up on the tables: my cue to pay and leave. Outside, it's cold, but not too cold. Not as bad as I know it will be in a few weeks. I try not to think about that. I walk to the Museum Gardens, checking I'm not being followed, and wait for the last loiterers to go home: teenagers drinking cans of cider, men walking their dogs. When eventually I'm alone, I spread my sleeping bag on a park bench and curl myself into a protective ball. I'm safer here than I would be in a doorway or in many of the hostels, but it's difficult to sleep out in the open. My body remains alert and tense and, for what seems like hours, my mind whirs with reconstructions and recriminations – all the things I should have done, those I shouldn't. For the past five months, I've survived by deception, by telling people the stories I think they want to hear and that might make them reach into their pockets. My own story isn't easy to understand. I'm not even sure I understand it myself. And with each lie, I've grown less sure of who I really am. I'm losing substance.

Lost.

I must have fallen asleep, as I awake with a jolt, knowing immediately that someone is beside me, watching me. I keep my eyes shut, but listen intently. I hear breathing. A rustling sound. My body stiffens and my heart pounds as I prepare to run.

'Want a crisp?'

When I open my eyes, I see a slight woman in a cagoule perched on the end of the bench. I sit up. She holds out the packet. I shake my head. Inwardly, I sigh with relief.

'Cassie,' she tells me. 'I'm an outreach worker.'

I rub my eyes. 'I don't need to be reached, thanks.'

The woman shrugs. In the early morning light, I see that she's small and wiry, perhaps twenty-five years old, with a smattering of freckles over her nose. For a while, we sit without speaking, the only sounds the singing of birds and the crunching of crisps.

'How old are you?' Cassie asks eventually. 'Seventeen?'

I don't answer.

She screws up the empty packet. 'Too young to be sleeping out, anyway.'

Still I say nothing.

'You don't have to do this, you know,' she says quietly. 'There are other options.'

'I'm not a charity case,' I say. 'I just needed to get away for a while. Clear my head.'

She nods. 'Sure.'

I can't tell whether she's patronising me. 'I can look after myself.'

'No one's saying you're not capable,' Cassie says after a while. 'It's just that, occasionally, we all need a bit of help.'

I think of my father and his reaction when my school tried to intervene. '*We don't need help in this family. We manage on our own.*'

Yeah, because that had worked out so well.

I look at Cassie and realise she's staring at me. It feels uncomfortable: as though she sees through me, past the mask, to the frightened little girl.

'What do you think?' she says. 'I can make some calls.'

#

I'm standing outside the front door listening for sounds from within, too nervous to ring the bell. Just as I decide to turn and leave, a woman opens the door carrying a black bin bag. She wears a bright red t-shirt and blue jeans, the legs ironed flat at the front like my mum's.

'You must be Sam,' she says. 'I'm Pauline. Come on in.'

She smells of scented soap and she jingles as she walks – gold earrings tinkling, gold bangles dancing on her wrists. She shows me into the kitchen and makes me a cup of tea in a rose-patterned mug while her husband, a thick-set man called Richard, tells me about the two of them: about how their kids have, 'grown up, grown wings and flown the nest,' and how they don't much like an empty house.

'It's nice for us to have a young person about the place now and again, isn't it, Pauline? That's why we signed up for the scheme. So you mustn't worry about cramping our style.' He smiles, and deep lines open up in his face.

The tea is good and sweet, and it's satisfying to drink from a proper mug rather than a plastic or paper cup. Small things you miss. We sit at the kitchen table for some time, talking and nibbling at biscuits (from a tin, not a packet). I keep expecting Richard and Pauline to ask me questions about how I've ended up like this: homeless and directionless, reliant upon the kindness of strangers. But they don't ask the questions I don't want to answer. Instead, they give me a tour of their house, with its magnolia walls, scatter cushions and silver-framed photographs of their children and grandchildren. I can't quite believe they'll let me stay here.

I think of my parents' house, which is in many ways similar to this one. Only there are no photographs in silver picture frames, or in any frames. There are no pictures. A sharp feeling of sadness pierces me. Homesickness: to be sick of home. To be ill because of what's happened there, but to miss it nonetheless.

That evening, I shut myself away in Pauline and Richard's bathroom. I've tried my best to keep myself clean: showering in train stations or washing in public toilets, shivering and scrubbing over metal sinks. It's never been enough, though, to remove the residue of dirt and corruption that seems to cover me. Maybe that's what has camouflaged me: not so much an invisibility cloak, as a coating of neglect. Now, in the blue-tiled bathroom, I fill the tub with hot water and submerge myself beneath it so that I can hear the strange gurglings of the house and the sound of my own breathing, amplified. The warmth permeates and renews me, and I begin to feel more substantial. Almost human.

Over the next few weeks, I continue to shed my invisible skin. I talk to Cassie about my failed exams and shredded hopes. I don't tell her how it all began: with a boy plunging from a bridge and disappearing into the dark water beneath; with a feeling that I could have stopped him if I'd listened harder and looked closer; with a family subsumed by grief and guilt. My little brother. I do, however, tell her about the debt – about the thousands I've amassed on credit cards by buying designer clothing and makeup that I neither wanted nor needed, but which I was using to conceal the real me.

'You can't hide forever,' she says, and perhaps she's right.

I complete forms; I make 'phone calls; I worry that people will see through me and realise I'm worthless. Eventually, however, I'm offered a place on a criminology course, and I get a part-time job in a bookshop to make a little cash. There, when I ask for money, people hear me.

It's six months now since I disappeared. Gradually, my mind is clearing. I'm beginning to remember who I am. Part of it is the counselling Cassie arranged for me; part of it is knowing she cared enough to arrange it. She's also helping me to find a flat of my own. Not that Pauline and Richard seem in any hurry to get rid of me. They've been kinder and more welcoming than I could have imagined. When I came down for breakfast this morning, Richard was sitting with his mug of tea at the kitchen table, still in his pyjamas and slippers, his grey-brown hair standing up in tufts.

'Late night, was it?' I asked, helping myself to cereal and sitting down opposite him.

'You know, Sam,' he said, blowing on his tea. 'You remind me a little of my own daughter sometimes. I'll bet your ma and pa miss you.'

The payphone box stinks of stale urine and bleach. I could have borrowed Richard or Pauline's mobile, I suppose, but I don't want to use a traceable number. Not yet. For a couple of minutes I stand staring at the calling cards and old bits of chewing gum that people have stuck to the board above the receiver. Finally, I slide the money into the slot and, with shaking fingers, dial my parents' number. I have no idea what I'm going to say or how they'll react, but I realise I am smiling. There are five rings and then my mother answers:

'Hello?'

Richard Lakin
Facing the Music

An ice-cream van tinkled in the distance and Bob shivered, thinking his mind must be playing tricks. He'd read all about hypothermia and knew it slowed the heart and brought on hallucinations. He rubbed his eyes, worried he was about to see a fifty foot high cornet with a flake jammed in the top. His teeth began to chatter and he jigged on the pavement, stomping his feet. You didn't get used to it, whatever folk said. Bob shrugged deeper into his greatcoat, pricking the collar against the biting wind. His eyes leaked, the tears pooling quicker than he could blink them away. He told himself it was the cold that caused them.

Bob crossed a yard where kids had chalked hopscotch grids on the flagstones. He was surprised kids still did such things when there were computers and countless other indoor distractions. He stared at the chalk until the lines blurred and the years fell away. He saw a playground with girls skipping and boys blasting a battered football, using busted saplings for goalposts. Away to the side a smaller boy with a straight, carroty fringe and shiny scuff-proof shoes stood watching, always watching, his bitten-down fingers stuffed in his pockets.

Bob had always been one for maths. Maths and music were his favourites, but getting an instrument had been out of the question. His father said they didn't have the brass and told that lame joke at every opportunity, thumping Bob high on the arm and bruising him to make the point. It hurt. His father had boxed in the Army, had what he called a 'good dig.' He said Bob wouldn't last five seconds in a boxing ring.

'You've got muscles like knots in cotton.'

Sometimes Bob would cry and retreat into his room, but still he caught fragments of their conversation, raised voices through the floorboards. And his parents' chat always got louder and looser with the drink.

'He's a worry, I know that much,' his father said.

'He's not. You're fussing Brian. He's just sensitive, that's all,' his mum replied.

'He's a wrong 'un, with his music and his funny books. I'm telling yer.'

'Just leave him be, Bri...'

'They tend to be good at it, though don't thee?' his father said.

'Who does?'

'You know what I mean. Their type's got a gift for that arty stuff.'

He'd go to the toilet and Mum would think she'd heard a creak and shush his father and slam the living room door so the frosted glass in the panel rattled. Mum was worried about all the 'carry on' with Bob's music and tried to steer him towards maths. One Christmas Bob was given a navy blue tin with Oxford Instruments written on the lid. As he opened the present his father shook his head, cussing that what Bob should really want for was a football or a pair of boxing gloves.

'I'd had six bouts when I was your age. You're not normal.'

Bob's tin went everywhere with him and people thought him strange, wondering why he preferred a set-square or a compass to a bike. One day Harris had waited for him after games and shoved Bob against the wall so hard his breath left him and the rough bricks scraped at his knees and knuckles. The tin tumbled from Bob's bag and Harris jumped up and down on it, crumpling the lid. A small group had gathered to watch Bob's humiliation. He stood facing the brick, wouldn't look at them. When they left, laughing and jeering, Bob picked up the broken, rattling tin. His hands were shaking. He stretched his mouth, fish-like to hold back the hot tears that made his vision swim. He opened the battered lid with a click and the contents – shards of broken ruler, protractor and set-square – fell out. Only the compass was left. Bob stuck the point in his thumb. It pricked the skin and a tiny bubble of blood formed. Miss Hastings watched from the window, obscured by winter sun. She kept a close watch on him in class that afternoon. The next morning, when they'd sung their hymns, Mr Hassall called for attention and said someone was to be the recipient of a special prize. Life-changing, he called it. Miss Hastings stepped up and plucked a folded tab of blue paper from a top hat while Mr Hassall built up the tension with a drum roll. Bob stared at the woodblock of the assembly floor, pleading, begging and offering up a silent prayer that it should be anyone but him. Miss Hastings held up the paper, unfolded it and said, 'The lucky winner is.....Robert Myatt.' His cheeks burned as he was called. He sat still, hands wedged beneath his legs, hoping they'd call someone else. They ordered him up and he learned he'd been chosen for piano lessons. The others glared at him. They didn't want the lessons, but it didn't stop them hating him for it.

Bob slid on the pavement and gripped a road sign, his heart thumping. The flagstones were sparkling with frost and the street felt as if it has been waxed beneath his paper-thin soles. Bob shuffled on.

Before long he had no idea how long he'd been walking. He held a palm to shield his face as headlights swept into the avenue casting him in spiky forty-foot shadows like a monster from a 50s sci-fi movie. He ducked through a broken fence with slats slick with green mould and waited, listening to distant sirens and the rattle of the railway carried on the wind. He pulled back a branch and saw a huge building with towering brick chimneys picked out against the moon. He scurried across the lawn, avoiding the tell-tale crunch of gravel and gripped a window ledge. He levered the window open with a blade, wincing as the wood cracked and splintered. He glanced over his shoulder but there was nothing except the rustle of leaves. He gripped the frame and scrambled in, tumbling through the window feet first into a broken sink blocked with moss. He rubbed his neck, sickened by the fall, biting back the urge to vomit. The toilet opened into a corridor lined with plastic chairs. A reception desk at the end of the corridor had a glass hatch and wire pigeon holes stuffed with brittle papers. Bob followed a corridor tiled like a chessboard. At the end there was a set of double doors. Bob peered through the doors and huffed on the porthole glass, buffing it to a shine with his elbow. Bob had slept in plenty of these buildings, unloved and forgotten, riddled with damp spores and crumbling plaster; littered with tell-tale clues of their past. He'd often found the same things as if there was a template for neglected offices and factories: calendars of topless women on paradise beaches, dog-eared index cards from the days before computers and dying cacti or spider plants hanging in cradles of parcel string. Bob squinted, struggling to see past the reflection in the glass. A smile played across his face. He grinned and his fingertips tapped out a rhythm on the door. He pushed through the doors, cracked his knuckles and walked to the stage, head bowed. He took a deep breath and stretched his trembling fingers as he climbed the steps.

'Get a grip, Bob,' he said and his heart raced. He sucked in a deep breath, tasting the dust. There was no stool so Bob folded a strip of fusty curtain and knelt before the grand piano. He blinked and swallowed. The trick was not to block bad thoughts but to let them pass like clouds. Bob licked his cracked lips. His eyelid flickered like a moth trapped in a lampshade. It was useless. It all came back to him. There were rows of expectant faces staring below him. His bladder was full, twitchy from too much sugary tea. His mother was wearing her best hat with the ribbon and the pretend cherries. It was a moment she'd been waiting months for. There was an empty chair beside her. She was glancing along the rows to check she was being noticed.

'Yes, our Bob, that's right.'

Miss Hastings coughed and whispered, 'In your own good time, Robert.' For Miss Hastings, in her mohair cardigans with the pearly buttons, he was always Robert. The fish in white sauce he'd had for tea was burning his throat. The stool was damp and itchy and Bob tilted from side to side, the way his father did when he tried to slip out a fart and blame the dog. Someone said something in the front row that punctuated the silence and there were sniggers. It was Harris grinning from ear to ear, relishing Bob's discomfort. Bob saw him among the chair backs and raincoats. Harris got to his feet, pointing and laughing. It took Bob a moment to realise what everyone was staring at. There was a puddle beneath his stool. It shone like a bubble of mercury on the polished, waxed floor beneath the stage lights. Bob ran from the stage, his scuff-proof shoes clattering on the boards.

Outside, in the car, Bob's trousers were itching. He was trying not to wriggle in the seat. He stared at the twinkling stars and wished he was up there, anywhere but here. His mother shook her head, seemingly too exasperated to find words. Bob tried not to scratch his thighs where they were sticky or to fog the window with his breath.

'Well, that's fifty pounds well spent,' his mother said finally.

The following morning Bob feigned sickness, pushing his porridge round the plate, till it stuck and gathered like putty. She sent him to school anyway.

Bob sighed. His mother was not here. There was no sign of Harris who was probably in prison or running a high street bank these days. The hall was empty. There was no assembly to laugh, no damp patch, no questions about wasted tuition. Bob ran a hand across his scalp. The carroty fringe had retreated almost to the crown. It was damp with sweat. Miss Hastings' words drifted from backstage.

'In your own time, Robert...'

Bob shuffled on the fusty curtain. He was rusty and it had been many years, but the notes came to him. Miss Hastings smiled and he nodded to her. He played better than he could remember. Tears came, but through joy, not through the cold or the ache in his chest. His shoulders dropped and, though music cannot fill a hungry stomach, for a moment at least he no longer felt the cold or the hurt.

Tim Tullet

Kurt

my life is brilliant - i am 'the invisible man'

i am homeless - i am alcoholic - i am an insomniac - i am suicidal - when you are where i am you look to the heavens for a reason to keep going - i look to the heavens where my radio signal comes from & find that Dotun Adebayo helps keep me going - & last night i found i still care about punctuation Dotun - it's strange the topics i hear on your program that remind me that - whilst i suffer - my mind still functions

i retrieved a newspaper from a skip last night to wrap around me for warmth - but i haven't been able to sleep - too many night screams here & not all of them mine - i am on a bench near a park light - i read a piece in the Culture section of the discarded paper by an American chap called Adam Johnson - 'Nirvana' - touchingly written - it has apparently just won the 2014 EFG Short Story Award - it touches - gently - on euthanasia - not an option for the poor souls like me who have no-one who cares whether they live or die anymore - & this weekend was the 20th anniversary of Kurt Cobain's suicide - he was only 27 when he pulled the trigger - it's strange that the piece i have just read name checks Kurt - life sometimes throws these small coincidences @ you - i don't know what finally drove Kurt to kill himself - perhaps he too heard someone describe him as being "@ the height of his peak" on air (as i did over the weekend) & wondered why as a crafter of words he bothered to carry on - when you are on the edge of the precipice it only takes one small push to fall - i occasionally wonder why i haven't been able to find Kurt's inner strength to help me end mine - i think it might have something to do with these words i found which have helped hold me up & keep me going ....

"sometimes even to live is an act of courage" - Seneca

i wonder why Kurt - a man who so eloquently described life & death & pain & anguish with such verve - with such 'courage' - couldn't find the courage to carry on ? - i just heard about the death of Mickey Rooney - he led a long & one assumes a full life - he has just passed away @ the age of 93 - reason takes no sides in this matter - you die when you die - i think i will try to give life another day - my time is not on me for a little while yet - @ least not today - i am off to raid the skips outside a major UK grocer - i hope to find some discarded food amongst the orange plastic bags - food which should find its way to the disadvantaged - the disadvantaged shouldn't have to find their way to the food - oh well - onwards & upwards - it's another day in

'Paradise' i suppose - & thank you again Dotun - you know not how many lives you touch & help

keep going - & i am one - my life is brilliant - i am 'the invisible man' - the invisible man

Katharine McLusky

Laura

I bumped into Laura last week. It was weird, like falling down a rabbit hole and winding up in your past. I walked into the meeting room, ready to present my designs for the website I'd been working on, and there she was, one of the clients. Turns out she's one of their support workers. We did the polite professional thing, then had a proper catch up over coffee afterwards. She looked great. Better than great. It was only after, when I sat down and thought about it, that I realised it must have been twenty years since I'd last seen her.

By the time I met Laura, Kurt Cobain was already dead. I was writing bad song lyrics about it. There was nothing to do in the village where I lived, so on Saturday afternoons I'd get the bus into town.

Often I'd meet up with my friends, but that Saturday they all had other plans, and I was bored. I wandered around, in and out of shops, flicking through CDs and clothes that I had no intention of buying, before heading back out into the autumnal chill. In the square outside the town hall a band was playing angry rock music, and I drifted over to join the crowd that had gathered to watch.

I lit a cigarette and drew the smoke down into my lungs, exhaling slowly.

"Pretty good, aren't they?"

I turned my head in the direction of the voice, and was met by a smile. She'd been talking to me.

"Yeah." I smiled back at her.

She was beautiful, with dark, elfin hair and green eyes, petite in a way that made me feel lumbering and clumsy.

"Can I be cheeky and ask you for a cig?" she said.

So that was why she was talking to me.

"Yeah, go on then." I reached into the pocket of my battered, second hand leather jacket and pulled out the packet, holding it out to her.

"Thanks," she said as she took one.

I pretty much expected her to wander off at that, but she stayed by my side, smoking and watching the band.

"I think they're raising money for the Samaritans or something," she said.

"Oh right, cool." I tried to think of something else to say. "I like your boots."

"Thanks. Oh hey, snap," she said as she noticed we were both wearing Doc Martens. Hers were cherry red, cooler than my basic black ones.

"Yeah." I couldn't think of anything else to say, so I smiled, and inwardly cursed myself for my lack of social skills.

We clapped as the band finished one song, then started another.

"Oh, I love this one," she said, and turned the full force of her attention on the band.

I watched as she bounced up and down, mouthing the lyrics. She looked so full of energy, so alive. For the next three minutes I might as well have been invisible. When the song finished she yelled her appreciation, clapping her hands over her head. The lead singer was definitely checking her out.

"Come on," she said, "I'll let you buy me a cup of tea. It's bloody freezing out here."

"Okay."

I trailed along beside her as she led the way to a cheap café, telling me about the music she liked – lots of bands I hadn't heard of, but plenty I had. It turned out we had similar taste. She ordered the teas, and I paid, then carried the steaming mugs over to a chipped formica table where we sat down. I hadn't liked to mention that I'd never had a cup of tea and didn't know if I'd like it. For this girl, I was a tea drinker.

The café was warm, with condensation misting up the windows and a pervasive smell of chip fat. The ashtray on our table was half full. I saw her staring at it, and offered her another cigarette, which she took with a smile. She lit it, then leaned over and very softly blew smoke in my face, before laughing, sitting back, and carrying on talking. I tried not to think too hard about how close her lips had been to mine.

By the time we'd finished our tea I had a pretty good idea about her views on politics (very left wing), feminism (pro), religion (anti) and TV (loving the first few episodes of X-Files, hated soaps because wasn't life miserable enough anyway).

"So," she said, "Thanks for the tea, but I need to head off. Places to be."

"Oh, okay," I said. "It was nice to meet you."

"You too. Look, do you want to go for a drink next week? You'll have to buy though 'cause I'm broke until the end of the month."

"Yeah, that'd be cool."

"Cool. I'll meet you here at half five next Saturday."

"Okay," I said.

She got up to go.

"Hey," I said, and she turned back to me. "What's your name?"

"Laura," she said, then left without waiting to hear mine.

I spent the next week wondering if she was really planning on meeting up with me, or if she was going to stand me up. Being stood up was the sort of thing that happened to me. By Saturday morning I'd almost persuaded myself not to even bother going, but there was a chance she'd be there, so I did my best with my hair, dug through my wardrobe for clothes she'd think were cool (eventually settling on army trousers and a long sleeved t-shirt), and got the bus into town.

Five thirty came and went as I sat in the café, nursing a mug of tea and smoking one cigarette after another. I didn't have a number for her, and she didn't have one for me, so if she'd wanted to cancel she'd have had no way to let me know. I sat facing the door, and each time it swung open I hoped, but it was never her. Fat women sat chatting, ignoring their kids who ran round and round the tables. Old men grumbled to each other. A bluebottle buzzed and bumped against the window. She wasn't coming. I hated the world.

At six thirty the café closed and I headed out into the cold and damp, drizzle that coated the streets with a thin sheen. I sat in the bus station and glowered at the world, glowered all the way home. I wondered why I'd ever thought a girl like that would want to know me.

I wanted to push her out of my mind, but the more I tried not to think about her, the more she was there, an itch I kept scratching and making worse. On Saturdays I dragged friends down to the café, always with one eye out for her. I hadn't talked to any of them about her, but I got a few comments about how quiet I was. Autumn edged relentlessly towards winter. I wrote songs about loneliness, pain and loss.

I was waiting at the bus station again next time I saw her. I noticed her before she noticed me, climbing down the bus steps, trudging across the concrete. She looked tired. I guess she must have felt my stare, because she looked up, right at me. I held her gaze. She walked over and sat down next to me, sinking into the metal chair like a deflated balloon.

"Hey," she said, her focus on the buses, not on me.

"Hey."

"Sorry I stood you up. Some stuff came up. I was kind of busy."

"Stuff?"

"My mum kicked me out – long story. I was looking for somewhere to live. Meeting random strangers wasn't exactly high on the priority list."

"Shit. Sorry. Are you okay?"
"Do I look okay?"
"You look like you could do with a random stranger buying you a drink."
I finally got a small smile. "Go on then, you've twisted my arm."
"I don't have ID though."
"Don't worry, I know a few places where they don't care."
Laura led the way through streets I didn't know, down to a dingy bar blasting out rock music. About half the kids there looked under age, so I figured we wouldn't have a problem getting served, and I was right – the guy behind the bar didn't look twice at me, just got me the ciders I'd ordered. We made our way over the sticky carpet to a free table in the corner and sat down.
"So," I said, leaning towards her to make myself heard over the music, "What happened with your Mum?"
"Can we not?"
"Oh, yeah, okay. But you have somewhere to stay?"
"Yeah, my brother's mate's flatmate is down in London for a couple of weeks so I'm crashing there for now."
"What about after?"
She glared at me. "What part of 'can we not' did you not understand?"
"Shit, yeah, sorry."
She picked slowly at the corner of a beer mat, gradually destroying it, watching the other people in the bar and not looking at me. I tried to think of a subject that might ease us back into a normal conversation.
"Um, so, have you heard the latest Manics album yet?" I asked.
"Yeah, my mate Dave's got it. It's pretty good. Kind of bleak. It's definitely better than the last one."
And with that, the conversation gradually started to flow again. I steered clear of anything too personal, and the more we talked, the more she seemed to relax. The bar gradually got busier, and the music got louder. A couple of guys came over to our table and tried to start talking to her, but she brushed them off. I was relieved.
We finished our drinks, and I offered to get her another one.
"Do you want to come back to mine instead? Well, I say mine, I mean Aaron's, but he'll be out tonight. I've got some vodka, we can listen to music…"
"Yeah, that'd be cool." I said. I didn't know if she was just asking me as a friend, or if there was something between us, but either way I knew I'd rather be alone with her than in some dodgy bar where guys would keep hitting on her.

We took a bus that wound through the hilly streets and dropped us off at the base of a tower block. She wouldn't take the lift, so we climbed flight after flight of stairs before eventually coming to the floor where Aaron's flat was. She let us in, heading straight to the kitchen area and grabbing a bottles of vodka and cheap coke, and a couple of glasses. I watched her pour generous measures of the vodka, topping up with the coke before she handed me my glass.

"Grab a seat," she said, indicating the sofa. "I'll stick some tunes on."

I perched on the edge of the sofa, sipping my vodka and coke, ignoring the too sweet, chemical taste, and focusing instead on the warm, relaxed way it made me feel. She flicked through a pile of CDs, eventually settling on one.

"Radiohead?" she asked.

I recognised the cover of 'Pablo Honey'. "Good choice."

As the sound of guitars filled the flat, she flopped down on the sofa next to me.

"I wish I could do this," she said.

"Huh?"

"Be in a band, be up on stage with all those people wanting to be me."

"You could totally do this," I said. "You're beautiful, I bet you've got a great voice."

"You think I'm beautiful?" she asked.

"Well yeah, I have eyes."

She smiled at me and I stared back at her like an idiot. Then she leaned forward, and very softly kissed my lips, pulling back to check my reaction. I leaned forward and kissed her back, as gently as she'd kissed me. She kissed me harder then, and it wasn't long before she was pulling me into the bedroom.

I let myself get swept along, lost in the moment. I let her tug off my long sleeved t-shirt, forgetting to be ashamed of my body. My skin puckered into goose bumps, from the cold of the unheated room and from the warmth of her touch. I let her guide my hands, felt the heat of her skin against mine. As the zinging guitar and ethereal singing drifted through the flat, she made me feel more alive than I ever had.

Afterwards, we lay under the duvet, with her snuggled against me, resting her head on my shoulder. I wanted to protect her forever. I stroked her hair softly, breathing in the mix of shampoo, perfume and warm skin that was her scent.

"I've never…" I started.

"Yeah, I could tell."

"Oh."

"Hey, it's not a bad thing. You're sweet. I like you a lot."

"I like you a lot too."

"Just don't tell me you love me or I'll run a mile," she said.

"Okay," I said. A little bit of the warm glow I'd been feeling faded.

She passed me one of my cigarettes, taking one for herself too, and lit them both. I inhaled deeply and tried to recapture the feeling of calm I'd had, but it had gone.

"So…" I started, but I couldn't think what to say next. I wanted reassurance, but I didn't want to look needy or clingy.

She traced her finger along the scars on my arm, and I wished I had my t-shirt back on.

"Why do you do that to yourself?" she asked.

The last time I'd tried to talk to any of my friends about that kind of thing, they'd got so frustrated with me that they'd told me to just go kill myself. I really didn't want that from her. She had actual, genuine problems. I was just me.

"It just makes me feel better," I said, giving her the short version.

"What's so bad that that makes you feel better?"

"Nothing. It's just in my head. I'm just not good at, you know, being happy and stuff."

"Maybe you should go see a doctor?"

"I did. They said I was just a normal teenager."

"Jesus. Sorry, but that's not normal. Go find a better doctor. Seriously."

"What about you? Are you getting help?" I asked.

"What, go put myself on a list to be stuck in some shitty B&B with a sleazy landlord? Get some goody goody breathing down my neck, telling me to drink less, smoke less, go to church? No thanks."

"So you're what, going to just stay at friends' houses? Then what? What about your future? What about school, uni?"

"I don't know," she said.

"Please at least go talk to someone."

"I will if you will."

"Promise?"

"Yeah."

"It's a deal then," I said.

"Okay. Now, distract me from all this depressing talk," she said, and started softly kissing my neck.

I felt the smile spreading across my face. I let myself get lost again.

She came with me down to the bus station so I could get the last bus back to my village.

"So," I said, "Want to meet next week?"
"Sounds good. Usual time and place?"
"Yeah. Let me give you my number in case you need to cancel."
I scribbled it on a bit of paper for her, and handed it over. She folded it and put it in her pocket. The bus pulled in, and the queue of people started to move forward.
"Next week then," she said, and kissed me, full on the lips, in front of everyone. An old lady tutted and glared at us. Laura rolled her eyes and kissed me again, then headed off. I took my seat on the bus, and watched her walk the length of the station, pale under the fluorescent lights, then out into the night, until eventually I lost sight of her.
The next Saturday I went to the café, got a cup of tea and a table facing the door, and waited. People weighed down with bags of Christmas shopping drifted in and out of the café. Couples talked and bickered, children smeared cake over their faces, waitresses complained about their feet. She didn't come.
It was about three months before I gave up entirely and stopped going to the café. I kept my promise, and went to see a different doctor, who sent me to a psychologist. Life dragged on. Months turned into years. I tried about five different antidepressants and eventually found one that helped. About ten years ago I stopped needing them altogether. I wanted to thank her. I wanted to know how she was. And sometimes, sometimes I just wanted to hold her again.
I'm not the person I was back then. I've had relationships and adventures, found new interests and lost some old ones. I don't think me from twenty years ago would even recognise me now. And yet here I am, sitting in a café at a table facing the door. I'm drinking coffee now, not tea, and I'm checking emails on my phone rather than just checking out the other patrons, but I still feel that tightness in my chest every time the door opens, hoping it's her, wondering if she'll show up.
When I saw her last week, she said she was sorry she'd stood me up, sorry we never really got a chance to get to know each other, but it was a really bad time for her. She said she'd got some help. She said maybe people weren't as bad as she'd thought. I said maybe life wasn't as bad as I'd thought.
I don't know if you can pick up where you left off. I don't know if she's interested in me, or if she can live up to the person I built up in my head. All I know is that it's five thirty, the door just opened again, and she's here.

Alison Hitchcock

A Seat on the Bus

As soon as I see the bus, that's when I get out my notebook and write down the number. I won't get on the bus until I have the number, written on a clean page in the top left hand corner. That's how Tom likes it done. I see Tom every day; he checks my work and makes sure I've had my dinner. He says that my work is a survey and that the bus company will be very pleased to have it, once it's finished. I don't know when it will be finished but Tom says I'm not to worry about that. Tom says I shouldn't worry about anything. But I do.

Bus number 11. Red. Singledecker.

I always keep my watch in my bag because it's safe there. The watch has its own special pocket. My mum gave it to me, and if I lost it I would worry that I might forget her. Tom says I'm not to worry about that. But I do.

9.45am

I show my pass to the driver.

"Y'right Graham? First trip of the day?"

I don't know how he knows my name; I don't know him. I don't say anything back because I need to be neutral. I can't show favouritism to any bus, otherwise the survey won't be right.

My seat is at the back. I like to have the same seat every journey. I always count the number of people on the bus. That doesn't include the driver; there is always a driver.

4 people

Girl – dark brown skin. Black hair. Yellow coat.

Man – pink skin. Black hair. Glasses with brown rims

Woman – pink skin. White hair. Pink jacket (not same pink as skin)

Man – grey skin. Brown hair - not much.

I can tell if someone has been sitting in the seat because there will be dents in the fabric and it will feel warm to my hand. There are no dents and it feels cold. If the seat had been dirty I would have brushed it. I have a brush in my bag for that. Usually I do have to clean the seat.

I pour hand gel onto my palms and rub them together until it has all gone. I put the hand gel back into my bag. My bag is heavy on my lap. I carry a lot of things in it. Tom says I don't need to take so many things out with me, but I do. My sister gave me the bag one day when she was visiting. She doesn't come very often since I moved into my room at the centre. She says that kind, brown ladies in India made the bag and mum would have wanted me to have it. The bag is brown as well and feels rough. I don't know if mum would have wanted me to have the bag. She always said she wanted me to have her house.

9.50am

The man and woman opposite are talking. She has a pink suitcase between her legs. He has a map in his hands.

Suitcase - pink

Map- green, blue, yellow, orange, red, black, brown.

It is important for the survey that I write down anything anyone says on the bus.

When do you move in with Petra?

rmm. The 10th". Yes, the 10th.

10th?

Mmmm. 10th.

It'll be nice. New home.

Just somewhere to live really.

Big is it? Her house

I guess

When do you move in?

10th.

Mmmm

There are a lot of pauses in their conversation but I don't know how to write down a pause. I don't think their conversation is very interesting but I have to write it down for the survey. My mum lived in a big house when she was little. She showed me a photo. It had a garden and a thatched roof. It was beautiful.

Once a girl sitting next to me was talking into her phone and saying I love you, Drew and I'm really sorry, come home. I was writing it down. She asked me what I was doing. When I showed her she got very angry and told the person on the phone and then I had to speak to him. He was shouting down the phone at me. She snatched my notebook and tore it up. There was a lot of noise. I don't remember what happened after that but Tom said that it all got sorted and that I wasn't to worry but that perhaps I should stop recording onversations. But I have to do it, for the survey.

The bus has stopped.

10.00am

New people get on.

Man – brown skin. Black hair. White headphones.

2 girls – pink skin – both. Yellow hair – both. Blue and pink nail varnish – both.

The girls sit in front of me.

They talk very quickly and it is hard for me to write it all down.

You see who's behind?
Yeah, I know.
Weird, innit?
What?
Him.
Yeah. Where does he live now?
Dunno. Surprised they let him out on his own.

My mum used to tell me about these sorts of girls; ones with short skirts and coloured nail varnish. Not good enough for you, Graham, she'd say, not good enough for my special boy. She said she'd find me a nice girl, to look after me after she'd gone, but she didn't. Perhaps she didn't know she was going. I didn't know she was going although my sister says I would have known if I'd have listened but I don't know what I was supposed to have listened to. Tom says I don't need to worry about what my sister says. But I do.

The bus stops again.

10.10am
No one off
One man on –yellow skin, blue trousers, white shirt.

The man starts to walk to the back of the bus. I think he is coming to sit near me because he is looking at me but then he stops and turns round and goes to a seat closer to the front. This is why it is important to have the same seat everyday, like I do, as then you don't get confused about where you are sitting.

Even though no one else gets on, the bus stays at this stop. It stops here every day. It should stop for five minutes. I have a stopwatch on my watch so I set it.

Driver reads newspaper

There is a park across the road. A woman is walking a dog. The dog is brown. A lot of dogs are brown. My dog was brown. She was called Floss. Floss went when my mum went but Floss went to a farm. I have a photo of Floss on my bedside table. I look at it every night. It is in a white plastic frame. There are two photos but the other photo is of a daisy in a field. It came with the frame. I don't have another photo that is the right size to put in the frame. My sister gave me the frame when I moved into the room. She said it was a room-warming gift.

There is a banner tied to the park fence. 'Summer Fayre here. Saturday 9th July 2pm. Help raise money for St Catherine's Children's Hospice'

My stopwatch goes off.

10.15 bus hasn't left
10.15.30 bus hasn't left

10.16 bus still hasn't left
10.16.30 bus still here
10.17 bus driver turns engine on
On - Woman with 3 children
Woman – brown hair, glasses, pushchair
Child – yellow hair, blue jacket, white socks, white sandals with mud on them
Child –smaller, brown hair, glasses, blue jacket, white socks, blue shoes
Child – very small, no hair much, pink coat. Being carried by woman.
10.20 – bus leaves

The bus has left five minutes late. The driver was ready to leave but the woman and children made him late. Being on time is more important than letting late passengers get on. The woman has sat at the front of the bus and she is talking to the children but I cannot hear what she is saying so I can't write it down. I'm glad that the bus survey doesn't need me to guess what they are saying because that would be very hard to do and I might get it wrong. Tom says that I shouldn't worry about writing things down wrongly. But I do.

The child with yellow hair is now standing on the seat. He has mud on his sandals. I want to tell the woman to make the child sit down so that the mud will not make the seat dirty but I don't want to shout because shouting is noisy. I get my brush out of my bag because if the woman sees me holding it she might ask if she can borrow it and then clean the seat. But she is facing away from me so she doesn't see the brush. The child standing up in the seat is facing me.

Child -sticks her tongue out.

The two children are now running up and down the bus. They are laughing and screaming.

When one child runs towards the back of the bus, the other runs towards the front. When they pass they collide. Usually the smaller one falls over. He doesn't cry. They squeal as they run towards each other and laugh when they collide.

Arrrr urrrrrr grrrrrrrr. A lot

I don't know how to write noise. I don't think that the driver has heard them because he hasn't stopped the bus. If there is a lot of noise on the bus, I think that the driver should stop the bus.

Now the two children are running to the back of the bus. The two girls are laughing at them.

They're so cute

Look at that one eating her lolly. It's all over her face. Ahhh

They run to the front and then to the back again. There is mud on the bus floor. It's very dirty but I cannot clean it because I don't want to get up out of my seat when the bus is moving.

One child is running towards me. She trips and falls. Her lolly flies through the air. It is on my notebook. It is chocolate and ice cream and it is stuck to the page. The ice cream is dripping onto my writing. The words are disappearing under the runny liquid. It is yellow and brown. I see lots of colours- yellow and brown and blue and white and black and red, and green … there is a screaming noise in my ears. I put my hands over them but it gets louder. The colours get brighter. The noise gets louder. More colours, swirling, splodges, everywhere. The noise hurts my ears. It's too loud, too loud, too loud…

***

I am on the floor and above me I see the driver's face. I can't tell if he is smiling or not.

"Y'right Graham?"

He offers me his hand but I don't want to touch him. I sit up. I am sitting in the mud on the bus floor.

"You just sit there, mate."

I am looking down the bus. The passengers are standing in the aisle or turned round in their seats towards me. I don't know why they are there but the bus is not moving so I don't suppose it is dangerous for them all to be standing and not facing the right way.

"Where's your mobile?" the driver asks "I'll give Tom a ring for you."

I look around for my notebook. I should be writing this down for the survey because I should write down everything I hear on the bus. I cannot see my notebook. I cannot see my bag. I cannot see my watch.

The woman with the children is standing next to the driver and she is holding my phone and passing it to the driver. The child, the child running up and down the bus, the child with the lolly, the child making a noise, is standing between her legs. The child looks scared. Perhaps she has been told off for running and being noisy on the bus.

The driver is now speaking into the phone.

I try to listen and remember what he says so that I can write it in the notebook later.

"Yeah, mate, just along Rushton Drive… yeah, we'll wait till you get here. No, no broken bones I don't think. Yes, he's come round now. Poor sod."

I look back at the passengers. Now they have gone back to their seats and are facing forward. Only the woman and the child are still standing in the aisle. She hands me my bag and takes hold of the child's hand and turns to go back to her seat. I smile at her but she doesn't smile. Perhaps she is angry because the child has lost her lolly.

I find my watch in my bag. 10.31.The bus should be moving along the High Street by now; not still here.The bus will be late when it arrives at the depot. I will write it in my notebook. My notebook is not in my bag.

"Come on Graham, come and sit at the front for a minute."

The driver has put his arm under mine and pulls me up from the floor. I don't want him to touch me. I can feel my body aching when I move. I have felt like this before but I can't remember when.

I look at the people sitting on the bus. I don't think that I have them all in my notebook. They are all looking forward. No one is speaking, which is good as it means that I have less to remember.

The man on the front seat moves his bag so that I can sit down. I thank him. He doesn't look at me. He pulls his mac closer into him, off my seat.

I check the seat. It is warm, so I get my brush out of my bag.

"Come on Graham" says the driver taking the brush from my hand and putting it into my bag, "let's just sit down, shall we? No need for all that today."

I see Tom getting on the bus.

"Hey, big fella." Tom always says that when he sees me. Tom is smiling. I like it when Tom smiles because then I don't need to worry.

"Come on, let's get you back. Just stand on the pavement whilst I have a word with the driver."

I get off the bus. 10.35.

From the pavement, I can see the passengers staring at me through the windows. I don't know why they looking. They're jealous cos you're a handsome lad, my mum used to say, that's why people like to look at you, Graham. I used to go to the zoo with my mum. The monkeys were behind the glass screens and they would stare at us for ages. And then they would suddenly get up and turn away, showing us their bottoms. How rude, my mum used to say, how rude. And then we would both laugh.

***

I am walking with Tom to his car. It is a blue car with silver wheels.

The bus goes past us. 10.40. Tom waves to the bus. I don't wave as that is favouritism.

"You OK big fella?"

I tell him that I am worried, as I don't know where my notebook is and I have to finish the survey. Tom says that I should have a rest from the survey for a while. He says that it will be for the best if I stay in my room for a while and don't go out on my own. I see that Tom is holding my notebook, my notebook for the survey. Tom says that he will hold on to it. He says that he has ripped out the page with the ice cream and chocolate stains on it. This means that he has ripped out the page with today's notes. I don't know what I will do for the survey for today but Tom says I am not to worry about that. Tom says I shouldn't worry about anything. But I do.

***

From the window of my room I can see the buses go past. There are a lot of buses that pass my room. I can write down their numbers, and whether they are single decker or double decker; and their colour; and what time they go by. I can't see who is on the bus or hear what they are saying. It is a different kind of survey now: a smaller survey. Tom says that the bus company won't mind.

I like looking out of the window. I like to see people going past. Sometimes kids come to the window and laugh and wave. I wave back. In the afternoon the sun shines into the window. I can feel the warmth on my face. It always feels nice. When I am in my room I cannot hear the noise outside, even though I can see the people and the buses. It is quiet in my room. Perhaps I will enjoy doing the bus survey from the window.

When I told Tom my idea to do the bus survey through my window he smiled and said it was a great idea. I like it when Tom smiles because then I don't need to worry.

Bus number 11. Red single decker.
9.45am.

Lilian Hope

Homeless

A True Story

It is early May 1991; I am standing under a large Oak tree wearing a vintage Phool dress surrounded by a vast expanse of yellow oil seed rape fields. The equally large blue sky is endless. The world seems to stand still, I feel like I am in a painting, the heavy smell of the flowers is intense, reminding me that this is real.

I am homeless. I am 22. I am pregnant.

This is my story.

Following the breakdown of an unhealthy turbulent relationship with my child's father I had turned up at my parents house, which I had left almost 5 years ago, it was a ridiculous idea as my teens had been a constant battle between myself and my father. I was trying to remain true to my developing bohemian character and personality with a father whose mission was to create a submissive, obedient daughter. He was driven by the word "reputation" as a leader in the church he believed it essential to be seen to manage his family, an unmarried daughter expecting a child was incompatible with this.

I didn’t tell my parents I was pregnant, my mother guessed and she was upset. Leaving me at home with my dad I faced a heavy lecture, I was offered two solutions; an abortion, so that no one would ever know, or a public confession that I had sinned in creating a child out of marriage, like God, he could then forgive me which would need to be witnessed by the church. Meanwhile my mother sought support, solace and advice from her work colleagues. I didn't wait to see if she would support me - I ran - I had one goal in my life to create a peaceful, safe womb for my unborn child, this was the one focus of my life and I doubted this was to be found with my parents. The new life inside me motivated me to put myself in a good environment; nothing had ever inspired me to fight so hard for safety. In a way this baby saved me.

I felt lucky to have recently made friends with a busker who let me stay in his vehicle where he lived with his wife, 2 year old son and Jack Russell, I felt accepted by these kind people who shared both their food and home with me. Together we travelled East through the vast yellow fields towards Cambridge where the busker knew he could earn good money playing his violin with the little dog "dancing” on her hind legs.

We park up at an established site on the Roman Road just outside of Cambridge where I soon meet people who know my ex, they were gathering their vehicles to travel West I decide to go with them leaving my friends behind I am expecting a quick visit, a discussion with my ex- hopefully some support. All I take is a change of clothes and an orange. I have no money.

When I arrived at the Chipping Sodbury festival I soon found my ex but I am alarmed to find he is selling ecstasy to teenagers, I decide I want nothing more to do with him I am aware this is not the environment my unborn child should have either now or in the future, this is in fact the last time I ever saw him. I have no idea how to get back to Cambridge all I can do is stay on the bus I travelled on and hope the people I am with decide to return soon, but they are not rushing back, my 'home' becomes a small space on the floor of a vintage bus with a variety of men I don't know and another Jack Russell. Nothing is demanded of me but I begin to feel anxious, overwhelmed and withdrawn- there is nothing familiar to hold on to, I had never been to a festival like this before, and I am not even sure where we are.

The police begin to chase us around the county determined to break up any further festivals and particularly to keep us away from Glastonbury and Stonehenge. They try to keep vehicles in small groups of five their gleaming white vans encircling the eclectic mix of buses we are travelling with, choosing to wake us in the early hours demanding we move on. Five police to each vehicle intimidating us with a bullying manner, we become united in our survival. We become supportive to each other. I have to get used to being searched because of where I am and who I am with. Shops refuse our custom and the few who let us in follow us around suspiciously. My situation is seen as a lifestyle choice so I get little sympathy when I try to get some income support. In Bath the Doctor refuses to see me when he realizes where I am based, the PDSA refuses to help the dog when it is discovered we have no address, locals see our sites as perfect places for raves they leave vast amounts of rubbish, noise and bad press. I try to keep the sites clean by asking police for bin bags, I try to keep my dignity by washing in public toilets watched by the shoppers who all seem to look like my mum.

I am becoming drained by the daily struggle to exist, my strength, bravery and focus are fast disappearing to be replaced by an all too familiar numbness, an inner switching off- a way I'd discovered years ago to protect myself during times when the present was unbearable. I was becoming a shadow woman, my spirit had gone elsewhere, this was the only way I knew how to survive- I went days without speaking. I was, however, pulled into the present by two things my need to eat and knitting. Knitting was taught to me by a woman on one of the sites, she made socks as a way to earn money- I lost her when the police split us into small groups so I never learnt how to make anything other than squares but the repetition and focus of each stitch kept my mind from disappearing completely. My hunger and the need to feed my unborn child left me no other choice but to become a skip hunter, I trailed round the back of shops going through their leftovers; mouldy hummus at Marks and Spencer's a slashed baby grow at the back of Mothercare.

Constantly moving was exhausting and unsettling I was grateful when we were pushed into a green lane in Hampshire near a quaint, thatched village and able to settle for a while, there were trees along the side of the lane supplying ample wood for a fire pit where I was able to make hot food and instigate communal cooking by encouraging people to bring any food however small, or wood and I would create a meal to share. Someone even provided a chair for me to sit in while I cooked which gave me great pride, it felt good to have a purpose. But my world was transient and while hunting for food my chair was used for fire wood and while hunting for wood my food supply was often stolen.

On the longest day, also my 23rd birthday, I found a small triangle of wild flowers growing strong and upright; poppies, cornflowers, large daisies, feverfew. It was beautiful. I was reminded that it was summer and as I sat there I saw a young woman long blond hair freely flowing behind her as she effortlessly rode bare back on a white pony along the line of trees that bordered the green lane. It felt like I was dreaming- she wasn't part of my world- completely out of place, my reality was a site filling with revellers, mouldy skip food lay strewn about under buses; dogs fighting over it, naked toddlers crying in the mud that was forming from a few heavy downpours. Extra people appeared on the bus who I didn't know they begun to experiment with all that the 1990's party scene had to offer the site was fast becoming a big festival.

As more and more people came onto the site the Police tried a new tactic- if we left the site for water or food we would not be allowed back on, terror threatened to overpower me. Trapped, I began to panic that I wouldn't be able to sustain a healthy inner environment for my baby without these basic things. People came from a charity with supplies of bottled water and oranges I begged for help, I was so scared. My situation threatened to drown me with its hopelessness. I couldn't see a solution until I saw a woman I recognized from Cambridge, she told me my busker friends were still on the Roman Road. She was heading back that night, with my rucksack of knitted squares, I took the long journey back East in a normal car without any bother from a single policeman.

Reunited with the busker and his family we headed towards Norfolk eventually settling in Lincoln between the canal and the railway line. There was only one other bus parked up and a bow top; we were also near people who were living on the canal. I befriended a man who lived on a boat with his 18 month old son; he was looking for someone to help with childcare so he could travel on the canal up to York, feeling I was in the way of the family I was staying with I decided to travel with this man, it seemed a good idea at the time.

We headed North with a Viking flag flying on the bow, I didn't have to work the locks and the childcare was easy, the baby was happy to sit on my knee as we moved slowly up the country but I quickly became wary of the boatman, he became aggressive demanding food from me- what little we had soon festered in the belly of the vessel, I was both hungry and incredibly thirsty. The man took to robbing vending machines in factories as we travelled. I didn't ask questions. I began to feel that I was with a dangerous stranger his mood was often dark and heavy, I feared he would kill me and throw me overboard if I challenge him on anything, the only ally was his small son and Alsatian.

I had walked into another nightmare and was weary of adventure, we crept along the water slowly, meeting no one, I felt incredibly lonely- his increasingly violent outbursts were unpredictable, but regular, always aimed at me never at the child; over simple things like yellow broccoli or if I drank any of the water. Anger seemed to constantly bubble beneath the surface- it took very little to spark an outburst. I hadn't seen this side of him in Lincoln. I took to sleeping on the towpath just to keep out of his way but always returned in the day as it was the only base I had in my small thread of a life.

I took no comfort as we approached Leeds, despite having spent a lot of time there when I first left home at 18. In York I felt terribly sad as we moored up in the centre of the city just beneath the bridge where I had crossed so many times in recent years when going to explore the vintage clothes and record shops. Memories of childhood holidays walking the walls with my family seeped into my mind, the beauty of the swathes of daffodils that had impressed me on so many happy visits to this city. Only the year before I'd felt so honored to be part of an excavation close to the Minster as part of an archaeology employment training scheme. I didn't want to leave the boat and go into the city while my life felt to be in such a mess- I felt disconnected, drained, and fragile. I knew how visible we were to the tourists as they crossed over the river on their way into the city; I knew they would look below them at the boats as they walked. I thought of how they would be imagining the romance of our life a total contrast to the actual facts.

As we approached Selby, on our return, I began to feel ill with a fever. I was terrified I was going to lose my baby; despite the fear I had at seeing a doctor I had no choice. I took the dog with me fearing that if I didn't the boat would have gone on my return, The Doctor and the patients were kind to me sensing my anxiety I was able to go to the front of the queue and given antibiotics for thrush and a urine infection. Back on the boat I was met with predictable anger, I just tried to keep out of the way trying to be as invisible as possible.

Returning to Lincoln I found my friends had moved on, the tension on the boat was unbearable, my daily challenge was to keep as calm as possible. One night I asked if it would be ok to let the stove die down before sleeping in the living area then went to sleep but in the early hours the boat owner woke me demanding I restart the fire as he was hungry and I made the mistake of saying no. The force of his physical violence threw me to the other side of the boat. I waited until he was asleep then I gathered the few things I had and pushed them in an abandoned shopping trolley taking the short walk into the city centre with no idea what to do or where to go just the knowledge that I had to leave.

It was a quiet sleepy Sunday morning. I found a derelict shop, the sort with a display window either side of a central doorway, and there I sat. I had 20p and a rucksack with a few knitted squares, a slashed Mothercare baby grow and a handful of clothes. No water. No food. No hope. The world woke up and people walked along living their lives, I felt dead inside-a ghost woman- thoroughly invisible. I was numb. I had nothing and no one and nowhere.

Opposite me was a phone box but I couldn't think of who to ring. I wanted to be safe but I didn't know how. I saw a phone number for the Samaritans; I looked at that number for a long time before finally ringing it. The person on the end of the phone told me some directions to follow and I was soon welcomed into a small room where I was given a plate of custard creams and a mug of sweet tea. After a long time of talking and being listened to I was given a space in a women's refuge. I had a bunk bed in a room with an older woman and her 14 year old daughter. There was a door that locked a kitchen to cook in and an immediate community of women all from very different backgrounds but all taking sanctuary in this quiet, peaceful place. A hint of hope flickered within me and in my womb my baby kicked for the first time.

Wiktor Kostrzewski

Synek

"Getting used to living in the United Kingdom can be a shock unless it's done gradually."

I don't yet know that last word, so I raise my hand and my teacher guesses my question, but makes me ask it anyway just to practice.

"Gradually," she says and repeats it so we all hear it. "Step by step." And then, being the child of the 90s, she launches into that NKOTB chorus. Nobody laughs.

I guess you had to be there. That was a year ago.

STEP ONE: Grandpa dies. As they unplug him and take all the pipes out, in comes a guy with a trained solemn face and a business card for a funeral parlour. Standard practice around here.

"Don't give me that," I say. "I'm seventeen." He looks around. There's nobody else. He puts his black hat back on. "Who's going to bury him then?"

"I don't know." He sticks the business card in Grandpa's pyjama pocket and sneaks out.

STEP TWO: An uncle says goodbye to me on the coach stop. It's a summer afternoon and the heat just turned into a storm. He says his wipers aren't working, so he'd best be off and will I say hello to mum and dad. As he runs back to the car, I see the coach pull up. The driver jumps out, expecting to help me pack. Big furry eyebrows raised at the size of my backpack.

"That's all you got, *synek*?"

We're off to London. Time to revise; I choose "Riders on the Storm," aptly.

STEP THREE: Mum is shaking and sobbing a little as she hugs me on Victoria. Dad reaches out for the handshake and almost nails it the first time. We find the Tube and they do that funny thing of telling me all the things I would have seen if I'd been on the surface - trying to sound like they've been everywhere millions of times and are local experts, until we get home.

STEP FOUR: Home is a dump. Rent is cheap. Halls are crowded. Kitchen is shared. Rooms are small. I start a diary, in English, just to practice. That's how I know that the following was, actually, Night 5: I went down to the kitchen to find a kid with his fingers in our pickle jar. Gave him a fright, pickle jar smashed to pieces on the floor. Kid starts screaming, kid's dad shows up and starts screaming, then there's a whole hallway of heads stuck out of doorways. Then dad shows up. To show he's got a handle on things, he makes me clean it all up - then reaches for his leather slipper, proper Silesian style, to settle domestic matters with a good beating.

STEP FIVE: It's like hearing a song you long forgot about. Except it's a shit song. If I thought they'd be different over here - well, I didn't, all the while on the coach I felt they wouldn't be different. If anything, it's easier for them to get booze, bicker and blame me.

STEP SIX: July 14, 5 a.m. - I go through mum's purse. Don't touch money - I know they'd get me for that - I just pinch my Oyster card with a travel pass which mum used to get child's rides on. Thus equipped, I'm off.

So this is now: I'm eighteen, just been in London for a few weeks - and now it's my home. As in, there's no other home for me.

"You can quickly find rules in British life if you are observant." "Miss?" "Observant - watching carefully."

Krishna van arrives, and there's no point pushing. You either get it or you don't. I'd like to see mum try to cook that. Fills you right up.

Then, up the road, there's a company with new offices. They've got a staff cafeteria on the ground floor, and a delivery room across the road. I walked past the cafeteria twice; that was enough. The staff spoke my language, which meant coffee. And the delivery room guys could always use some help with boxes, which meant using their shower to scrub myself, and my change of clothes, clean.

Every time I asked if I could come tomorrow. Except for Fridays when there was no point.

Up the road a bit, and turn left: There's an arts university with a sunny square.

Steps covered with artificial grass lead down to a canal. This is where I take my naps and I dare you to tell me apart from the art students.

There are toilets in parks and art galleries. There are water coolers in banks and post offices. Libraries, museums are great when it rains, or when it's too hot. Except you need to look clean, otherwise there's trouble. I'm learning lots.

As for sleeping - I learned to pick the right night buses, and get a mid-day siesta. Tube was too loud for me. In the end, I slept about the same as I would back at the house.

The Oyster pass expired, and then you had to look at the gates for people with travel cards. If you asked, they sometimes didn't need them any more: that was your ticket then, and a night-bus ride, but you had to time it.

All this, and more, until the first frost showed up on windows, and my clothes got too thin and tired from washing.

"What does welfare state mean, Miss?" "Ah - hard to explain."

I'm getting an interpreter for my second meeting.

The most valuable thing I got from the first one was a refill on my water bottle and a toilet trip. Otherwise, the people at the council couldn't figure me out, and told me to go away. So I come back and demand an interpreter.

The man behind the desk sighs, picks up his phone - and in five minutes, we begin the phone ping-pong. He listens to the phone and talks back. Passes the phone to me. I listen to the interpreter and talk back. Pass the phone.

I actually understand the man behind the desk pretty well. I'm getting the interpreter for two reasons: to get more time to think about my answers, and to get an adult guy on the line and in my corner. I tell the guy on the phone this much, tell him not to interpret that. "You're not the first one," he scoffs.

Soon the nice man behind the desk starts telling me that there is very little he can do, and I know to ask questions and keep asking, until he remembers something he can actually help me with. But there is not much. Apparently, if you're from abroad and just over 18, they cannot help you and don't have to - at least for the first 3 months, and at least if you believe this guy.

"You must tell me why you refuse to go back to your family and work things out."

I pass the phone back to him, lift up my T-shirt. See, it's been a while; anything less than expert-level scars should have healed by now. I say loud enough for the interpreter to hear:

"Tell him that this is how things work out when I'm back there."

This just completely confuses the poor desk guy, who can only repeat how there's nothing he can do.

I'm just about to hang up, when I hear the interpreter speaking out of turn. "Hold on, *synek*."

Synek - that's "sonny" where I come from. Anybody can be anybody's synek when they're young. He's from my part of the world, and he wants me to hold the line. He silences the office guy with one or two things - can't really hear what exactly - and the next thing I hear is him tapping away and, I think, googling maniacally.

"You there?"

He comes back with something. I'm asked to remember the uncle's address. Then I'm told to pass the phone back. This whole thing takes forever, but in the end the guy on the phone comes back to me.

"You're flying back to your uncle. There's a charity that just helped us arrange this." "And this guy - didn't know about it? You had to tell him?"

The interpreter's next line refers to the desk man. Filthy and hard to translate, but then he tells me again:

"Hold on there, *synek*."

"Home is where your heart is. Do you understand that?" "I do, miss. The words, I mean."

The desk man has me come back to my address. At least he gives me the printed documents there and then. I have the cafeteria ladies keep them for me back in that office building.

"Going somewhere?"

"Home first, and then back home." "Excited?"

"Hmm."

There are five days to go. Five days and nights. The first night is the worst. After that, I just show my face to mum and dad every now and then. Take a shower, change clothes. I still catch naps in libraries and on night buses. I still get the Krishna van and the free coffees. Sitting on the fake grass by the canal, I still look like an arts student. And with all the art galleries I've been to, I feel like one. When it's too cold to ride - or during that one weekend that I must spend in, no point sleeping on night buses on Saturdays - that's when I sit in the attic, staring out the window, looking at the planes. Mum and dad drink or fight downstairs. I'm four feet above them.

In another story, I could hold them and we could talk and maybe move out of here or something.

In this story, I'm four feet away from a place called home - but it feels (thanks to ages of practice) very far away. There's a city out there that I never asked for. I wish it was summer and fake grass forever.

"We'll be learning from a song today. I want you to try to remember the words first."

Of course I tell them nothing.

An early morning bus to the office. This feels like going to work! I pick up my secret papers, a farewell cup of coffee and a hug.

It's a Tube and a train ride. I'm counting the stations, remembering what's at every stop. Changing at Victoria - where I came all these ages ago. The same guy sits there, playing the same four chords. Over and over again.

"What is that song and why don't you sing it?"

"It's Tracey Chapman, from 1988, man. I forgot the lyrics already. Something something revolution."

The train crawls out from the dark tunnels, over the river, to my first plane journey home.

Nina Aked

The Little Match Girl 2013

The little girl with the matchsticks by *Hans Christian Andersen* was first published in 1845

New Year's Eve, cold, the coldest day so far, except possibly for Christmas day when frosted stars transformed puddles into sparkling pools of light. The last of the songs were played out, the last of the drunks sang out for Christmas day. There were no well wishes, no exchanges of good will. All was still, save for the soft white billows of her breath moving though the darkened air.

Only days before there had been hope, presents and coins pressed into her hands and Christmas wishes from smiling strangers. She hurried back to the basement flat, happily. Her little brother jumped around asking what Santa had brought, the black stare of her mother's eyes answered. Her fathers' fist swept everything to the floor.

Snow swirled and formed feathered circles around the orange street lights. Flakes dusted her long hair, settling against her lashes. She pushed her hands deeper into her pockets, hoping to find warmth or perhaps a lost coin slipped deep within the torn lining.

She was invisible, pressed against the wall watching. Red sale banners proclaiming massive discounts obliterated the winter wonderland of gleaming lights, the tables laden with plastic roast dinners and the great window. Here children had gathered greedy eyed, to see the musical scene of skating snowmen and assorted absurdly dressed animals, surrounded by boxes tied with brightly coloured ribbon.

The manager scowled, muttering, beggars would put off the customers. Shoppers scurried past unseeing, their arms full of red bags proclaiming sale, sale, sale.

Before the snow she'd found a discarded pair of boots and slipped them on, they were unwanted, it didn't matter. They were far too big, still, warmer than her canvas shoes. Now cold crept into the space between her toes, nipping pinching.

Shop girls bustled past; one dropped a lighter, glancing back to dismiss it, her hands clawed around too many bulging carrier bags to be bothered to pick it up.

A firework shrilled, the girl looked up, purple and pink shooting stars twinkled into a trail of blue flame before dissolving into the thickening snow. Her hands tingled with cold. Maybe when the next hoard of alcohol fuelled merrymakers came to town they would throw a little change her way.

She picked up the lighter and flicked it, running her fingers through the fragile flame; she imagined slipping through the shop door, running her hands through the warm piles of clothes, cramming her mouth and pockets with chocolates and cakes. The heated plastic pressed against her hand, the flame sank and died.

She flicked again, a hypnotic yellow flame, at its heart a memory, cinnamon and cardamom spiced light. A face she remembered, soft creased cotton smiles, she closed her eyes remembering silken flour drifting though her fingers and the taste of spiced sugar. Her grandmother scolded gently as the girl dipped her finger in the warm cake mixture. The flame blinked and perished.

The road now seemed quite deserted, oddly quiet as if pausing for breath, waiting for people to return. She remembered a cartoon of a flying boy and a snowman, how great it must be to soar about the city, not to feel the cold noise and chaos of life. Now she remembered a voice, signing softly lullabies and a face looking over her, dancing in the golden light, an angel in a dream only half remembered.

Snow muted the city's voice to a whisper lullaby, lullaby, lulaby. She was weightless and warm, wrapped in the arms of her memory, her grandmother beside her. High above the city lights, together they shimmered brighter than jewels, around them the night sky spinning rainbows of perfect light. She remembered gifts given and shared, a knitted doll, a painted box, and remembered stories shared and laughing eyes.

Down below the weary world scurried by, shoppers sought elusive bargains; bin bags spilled crumpled brightly coloured paper and broken toys. A man dragged a forlorn and bare Christmas tree to the end of the road. A dust cart swaggered down the slushy street.

The journalist dressed in festive red stood outside the store, waiting for the director to shout 'Wrap.' Someone unimportant died, time to go home. She smiled at the camera. 'We would like to wish our viewers a Happy and prosperous New Year.' New Years' day, the story was done.

Dee La Vardera

No Big Deal

It's like sitting in the locker room before a match. Same smell of sweat and disinfectant. Same tight feeling in your chest just before you go through the door out onto the pitch in front of all those people. Terry Cocker sits on a bench in the holding cell where he is waiting to be taken up to court.

He's been told that the Magistrates in Court One are running late. Hundreds of motorway cases. 'That's the trouble with the M4 on our patch,' the duty prison officer informs him. 'They all turn up, you know. The defendants. Think coming to court dressed up in their best suit, correction, their only suit, wearing a fancy tie and polished shoes. Think the beaks won't disqualify.' He sighs. 'Court Two's offered to help out. ' He pats Terry on the shoulder. 'Sorry, mate, have to wait a bit longer.'

Terry always seems to be waiting for something. He has plenty of time to think about why he's landed again in this situation and what is going to happen next. But he's tired of thinking. He looks at the floor and counts the tiles then looks up and surveys the ceiling. Cobwebs in the corners. Black gunge along the edges of the strip lighting. He looks down and focuses on the names scratched on areas of the blue gloss walls. He feels no desire to add his own to this directory of desperation. 'Baz woz 'ere' 'Grinder4Ever'. Terry just wants to get it over and done with. Plead guilty, take the fine and bugger off.

But where? That's the trouble. He hasn't got anywhere to bugger off to. Sleeping on friends' floors (not many of them left). Dossing in sheds and barns. He thinks about the stupidity of it all – the whole system. Why spend taxpayers' money on prosecuting him for stealing a loaf of bread and a pint of milk? It'd be cheaper to give him the stuff and send him on his way. Homeless, penniless and a string of minor offences, it didn't look good. They wouldn't lock him up, surely, even if he had no permanent address. They wouldn't do that would they? Drunk and disorderly, urinating in a public place, the only recent offences on record. Nothing serious. And now, stealing a loaf of bread and a pint of milk. No big deal.

If only that stupid cow had let him sleep in her barn. That la-di-da, plum-in-her mouth, four-by-four-driving, golf-playing so and so. She had plenty of space, acres of land. He was nowhere near her house. If only the toffee-nosed bitch had slipped him a pound or two for a meal, or better still given him something to eat, instead of calling him all sorts of names and threatening to phone the police. Then he wouldn't have hitched back to town and wouldn't have been caught on the CCTV nicking a carton of milk and a loaf of bread from the back of a delivery van in the High Street. Lesson One - never leave open doors unattended. Lesson Two – just walk on. If only the van doors had been shut.

If only. His life story. If only he'd been able to find a job and stick with it after coming out of the army. If only he'd been a better husband to Kathy, and father to Tracy and Sam. If only his wife hadn't divorced him and taken the kids far away up North. If only he hadn't preferred the bottle to making the effort to keep in contact with the family. Could this be the final kick up the backside he needed? Plead guilty, take the fine and bugger off somewhere. No more doorways, hostels or fights. No more snotty people looking down their noses at him. Start again. New town. New faces. New beginning. Maybe give Tracy a call. He still has the number, scribbled inside the Father's Day card he'd kept from 2008.

As Terry enters the dock, he sees that the court is packed – all those motorists waiting to have their licences endorsed. It's a sea of dark suits and sober ties. Hard to tell the defendants from the solicitors. He rubs his hands on his dirty, creased trousers. He looks down at his shoes and notices the scuffs and stains on his boots. He wishes now that he'd taken the usher's offer of a cloth to polish them. Terry knows how to buff up a bit of leather till it shines.

When the Clerk reads out his name Terry turns to face the magistrates. There are two women and a man sitting on the Bench. Women are good, more tender-hearted. They've got kids. They know what it's like out there, the dangers and temptations. The man on the right is busy settling his chair and shuffling papers. He looks like a military man, something about his bearing that Terry recognises. The Guards probably.

Terry closes his eyes and lowers his head while the charge is read. The duty solicitor has rushed over to Court One to another case. In their brief talk in the noisy lobby, Mr Marshall recommended a guilty plea - 'Not to waste the court's time and thus a speedy expedition will go in your favour'. Protecting some businessman's licence is obviously more important to Mr Marshall now, than helping Terry keep out of prison. On your own, mate. What's new? Face the music alone. Guilty. What else could he plead? He was drinking from the carton of milk when the CSOs found him in the park. Not proper police he thought, but he wasn't going to argue with them. He'd actually said, used the words only TV villains use, 'It's a fair cop.' Got to laugh. He went along quietly. Pathetic really.

The female magistrate in the middle adjusts her glasses and turns her winged chair to face Terry. The Chairman of the Bench is addressing him directly. It suddenly registers with Terry who she is. It's the voice, that voice. The cut glass accent, the exaggerated enunciation. He dare not look up. It's that woman, the posh one on the farm. The one in the old waxed jacket and muddy wellies who shook her fist and shouted abuse at him. 'Get off my land you effing scumbag! This is private property. If you don't eff off now, I'll call the effing police!' The toffee-nosed bitch who chased him out of the barn is up there on the dais, all dressed up in her smart suit, wearing dangly gold earrings and matching brooch on her lapel. She is looking straight at him.

When she recognises him, she'll say something. She has to. Terry knows that she has to declare it. She can't continue hearing the case, can she when she knows the defendant? 'Prejudicial to the due process' it's called. He knows. He's heard the words before. His heart is racing. If she tells the court that she knows this man then she has to withdraw. They can carry on with just two, can't they? It doesn't matter if the Chairman sits this one out.

Or maybe they will decide to adjourn. Then he'll have to stay locked up. They won't grant him bail. They won't. No Fixed Abode. Won't let him off to wander around the countryside for a week, trusting him to turn up for the next court appearance. If she does declare an interest he's damned; if she doesn't he's still damned. She'll tell the other two when they retire to discuss the case, that she knows his sort. You need to teach these layabouts a lesson. Set an example. The press are in court and we need to send a strong message out to the public. Let the local community know that all thefts are treated seriously. Zero tolerance. Damned.

She looks straight at him, serious grey eyes unblinking, thin red lips tightly drawn. She gives nothing away. Does she see him at all? Is that it? Is he invisible? Does he actually exist to her as a person? Scumbags, drunks, and dossers look all the same to her.

He's meant to speak now. If he doesn't say something then his silence might be taken as insolence and make things worse. He doesn't want to look more guilty than he really is. The microphone is attached low down on the side of the glass screen. He will need to lower his head in order to reach it. How can he bear to hear his own voice echo round the courtroom, denouncing himself? I am Terry Cocker, drunk, wife-beater and thief. If he mumbles he'll only be asked to speak again but louder.

Everyone is staring at him. He feels so alone. He is truly invisible now. Just another criminal on the list. Where are the men he patrolled the oil fields of Kuwait with to stand up for him? Where are the lads he taught to identify detonators and devices for their tours in Basra? There is no one to stand up for him now. Whatever he says, he is damned as soon as he opens his mouth. So he keeps his mouth shut.

There is a sudden noise and a flurry of movement at the back of the court. Terry looks up to see Mr Marshall rushing in, pink tie flapping and pile of papers fluttering. He strides purposefully down the aisle towards the Bench. 'Apologies, your worships. Business in Court One.' He looks across at Terry and nods. 'I would like to say a few words on behalf of my client, Mr Terence Cocker.'

Mr Marshall offers Terry a cigarette as they stand outside the courthouse.

'Thanks for what you said in there.'

'Lucky they didn't adjourn for reports. £60 fine and £10 towards costs isn't a bad result.'

'Funny that,' Terry says. 'I can't even afford two quid for a pint of milk and a loaf of bread.' He stops to think about what he could do with £70. Get him to Nottingham for a start where Tracy's last address was. Maybe get to see his granddaughter. Take her a little present.

'They won't chase you up for the money for a few months. By the time they do, you'll be sorted, I'm sure.'

Terry laughs. 'Don't know about sorted.'

'You'll get back on your feet. My old man was army. I know what it's like. You can do it.'

Terry nods.

'Came out age forty-eight. Completely lost.' He looks up at the darkening late afternoon sky. 'Two years' later. Died of a heart attack.'

'I'm sorry.'

'You can only go up from here, you know.'

'It's a long way.'

'No distance at all. No big deal for a man like you. You're not the usual mindless yob I see every day. Pity people don't know how much they have to thank you for. '

He didn't need any thanks. Terry draws deeply on the cigarette and watches the smoke diffuse in the cold afternoon air. He is reminded of other times, catching a ciggie in a shell hole. He remembers when his men were caught in crossfire and how they did what they had to do without thinking. Automatic. Second nature. Well-trained. He smiles. He thinks of the time he carried Corporal Tyler away from a blazing vehicle, black-faced and bleeding. He didn't need any thanks. He could see it in the man's eyes.

'I'll take you up on that offer of a lift to Junction 15, if that's OK.' Terry takes a last few drags and treads the cigarette stub out on the kerb. 'See if there's a truck going my way.'

He turns for a moment at the sound of squealing tyres and sees a mud-spattered Range Rover reversing out of the Magistrates' car park. He watches the woman driver, half an hour ago the Chairman of the Bench, as she miscalculates the manoeuvre. She hits the bumper of a car, double-parked near the entrance, smashing its rear offside light. She pauses, hunches over the steering wheel and looks through the windscreen, scanning to left and right and then behind like a meerkat on the lookout for danger. Seeing no one, she slams down the pedal. With shards of orange plastic crunching under her tyres, she speeds off out of the gate and away up the road.

Olivia Gwyne

Heading North

Andy is moving on. He arrived hoping there might be work, but there is none. The hostels are full and so are the streets, congested with traffic and police, and people rushing everywhere and no one stopping. He has no connections here, and is tired of being afraid, day and night.

He gets on at a rail station with no ticket barriers and keeps an eye out for the guard. Travels up the coast and gets off while his luck still holds. He knows no one and no one knows him.

Outside a newsagents he overhears a conversation; there is a job in a kebab shop just off the front. He goes round there but the guy looks at him as though he is crazy. He knows that look; even if there was a job do you think I would give it to it you with your dirty jeans and knackered boots and a sleeping bag on your back.

At the bus station he studies the boards, to sees what time buses come and go, trying to look as though he wants to travel somewhere so that he can sit down for a little while under cover. Some suited and booted bloke comes over and gives him a bus ticket and tells him it's still valid for the rest of the day. On a map of bus routes Andy sees Deadtown, stuck at the edge of England, the end of the line. He has to keep moving so he gets on the bus and goes there.

Deadtown matches its name. It is dilapidated and careworn. He buys a bag of chips. Wants that hot, greasy feeling of satisfaction and a notice in the window says there are jobs at the fish plant, so he eats his chips and goes down there.

He sees straight off why they are putting adverts in chip shops windows, why they always have vacancies. Shit money and shit hours, and you smell of fish all the time. The foreman seems straight enough. He doesn't big the job up; it's hard work and minimum wage, and Andy can start the next day if he wants it. The foreman knows a bloke who has a room to rent in a house he owns.

When Andy gets there it is a flat with two other blokes. The kitchen looks like a bomb has hit it. The living room is not much better. There are old pizza boxes and empty fag packets. There is a fug of unwashed bodies and unwashed clothes and the goat stink of men who live together without the restraint of women. When he had a place of his own he liked to keep it clean and tidy. At least he has a room to himself. He can keep that clean and tidy, and make it his own.

He doesn't like the look of the other two much. They could be in their forties but it's impossible to say for sure. They are weather beaten and hardened; they could be any age. One is big set and full of chat, the other small and morose always looking to the other one to see if it is OK to talk. They have tinnies out when he arrives and invite him to join them. He says he's got a bad head from all the travelling and has to be at work at six the next day, so they let him be. He knows from experience that will not last.

Andy makes up nicknames for them; Lardy and Stumpy. They work at the fish processing plant as well. The three of them walk to and from work together.

Andy is tired when they walk to work in the pitch black of morning that feels like the middle of night. He is tired on the way home, when his muscles and bones ache.

Lardy is both talkative and nosy, wanting to know the far end of a fart; who you are, where you come from, all your business. Evasion makes him angry. Stumpy is weak and malleable, a bit depressed perhaps, always looking for someone to tell him what to do. Andy keeps quiet as much as he can.

There are lots of Poles at the plant. Some of them speak English quite well and Andy has a bit of a chat with them sometimes. He asks them what Poland is like and how they come to be here and what they think of it. They have come to work and to send money back, and they want to go home. All of them have plans for what will happen next in their lives.

They ask him what he will do with his life and he shrugs and says, I don't know. He can see them watch him and wonder about him. He is too ashamed to say, even with these men he will meet only here, the truth of his own life. Cannot even say it to himself.

Lardy and Stumpy are sounding him out. Every evening the three of them eat together. A pizza or fish and chips and one night some stew out of a tin. Every night he has an excuse not to go out and drink with them. He is tired or skint or feels sick after the endless stench of raw fish guts. They come back just gone eleven and he can hear them talking and laughing. The door has a lock but he wonders if Lardy has a key to the room, some of his things have been moved. He can imagine them in his room rooting through his things, looking for money. Andy has a body belt and all the money that he has is on him.

They let him be all week but by Friday night he has run out of excuses.

There is a pub on the worst looking stretch of road out of town, the Jolly Pirate. The pub is old, half-timbered, made ridiculous by the ridiculousness of its name. It may once have seen a pirate but Andy doubts it has seen jolly for a long, long time.

They drink in the back bar, pints of cheap bitter and lager. Some of Lardy's other cronies have joined them and they rib Andy, take the piss out of his short hair and his quiet ways. He suspects they have put vodka in his lager. Stumpy and some of the others are very drunk. They laugh loudly at Lardy's jokes and constantly ask his opinion and Andy sees that Lardy has become a reference point in a world where no one has any landmarks.

The bar is filling up and as chucking out time approaches the atmosphere starts to change. The laughter become crueller and the banter nastier and Andy sees tension and anger sparking and igniting.

The alcohol has kicked in. Usually he likes to feel drunk, it separates him from his life, makes things seem remote, better than they are, but not tonight. He wishes that he had somewhere else to go, a place where he could lock the door and be safe, be himself.

Fearing the alcohol will dim his senses when the trouble starts, and he will not be able to protect himself, he goes down to the bogs, and in a cubicle sticks his fingers down his throat. He gags a bit but has to do it several times before the reflex kicks in and his stomach contracts and the torrent of vomit gushes out. He spews until he has purged himself. There is a vile taste in his mouth and the burn in his throat is like fire.

He goes back to the bar, knowing that he stinks. As he sits down he says, bloody light weight, I've just chucked me guts up. I can't keep pace with you fellas.

They like that, he gets a bit of cheer and one of them buys him another pint. He's not a threat, he's just a kid.

The bar is rammed when they ring the bell for last orders. That's when the punch up starts. Some jostling at the bar, harsh words and harsher actions. Men fighting to keep their ground because that is all they have to keep. The trouble spills out into the car park at the back. Lardy gets himself in the thick of it, throwing his weight around, literally. Stumpy is the weasel at the side lines, goading, egging others on. Lardy and one of his mates get a man down and are kicking him where he lies.

In the midst of the screaming and shouting and blood spilling, Andy finds himself concealed in the shadows. Sliding silently along the pub wall, he makes it to the end of the car park. There is a low wall and he scrambles over it and is away. Runs, then jogs and then walks, but no one is behind him.

He's gone less than a 1000 yards when Lardy texts, where are you mate? All the lads back to ours for a few tinnies. That ginger barmaid and her mate'll be there!

Andy texts back. On a promise. See you later. Don't wait up!

Then he turns his phone off.

He sits down on a wall in front of someone's house. His head is banging. His stomach creaks and protests at the agony of the intensifying cramps. He is absolutely empty.

When the nausea subsides Andy wanders through streets he does not know and tries to think rationally about everything. He is going downhill, towards the harbour on slip ways and deserted streets and past derelict warehouses. In the distance he hears a clock chime twelve. There is not another soul to be seen.

But Andy knows in this so-called deserted part of town that by midnight there would be people who called it home. They would be sleeping in amongst the cardboard boxes and newspaper they'd found, and under dirty old blankets they'd carried all day. Hankering down for a few hours sleep, hoping for a few hours of escape.

Out of doorways and broken windows and the cold night air, he feels their eyes on him. As though all the ghosts of all the lost are watching him; old mariners and old soldiers, and destitute women and children, and all those living, hanging on at the very edges.

Andy keeps on walking, down to the waterfront. There is a sharp breeze coming off the sea, briny and acerbic. Sitting on a bench looking out to the great sea wall curving round the harbour he wonders how much longer he can keep this up; this drifting and never resting, this living from hand to mouth, this hiding and surviving. He is twenty years old and already there is a part of him that is frail and ancient, for whom everything feels as though it lies behind and very little lies ahead.

He knows it is not his time but he thinks about it sitting on the bench. Not the dark oblivion afterwards but the act of it, the rope cutting into your neck as it takes the weight of your body and the fight to hold down the painkillers and whisky and the rush of air and speed as the train hits you, all of you exploding with the impact.

Cold, he goes back up to the town centre and hunches in a shop doorway. It offers some shelter from the wind, but if he can he avoids sleeping out on nights like this. The ache of the cold is already inside him, in his fingers and toes and arms and legs, and it is too easy to nod off and not feel it slide into the marrow of you, so that you never wake up again. But this night it is the chill that wakes him, and he gets up and goes back to the flat.

Stumpy, the cronies and a couple of lassies are asleep, stretched out on the sofas and the floor, surrounded by empty cans. Lardy and the red-haired girl from the pub are sprawled across Andy's bed. There is semen smeared on his eiderdown.

He can see they have been through his things so he gathers up what he can, stuffs it in his back pack, rolls up his sleeping bag, and putting his door key on the table, leaves.

Maybe he will keep heading north. Maybe he will try Newcastle, or Edinburgh, or Glasgow.

Jax Leck

Homeless

Boot to ribs, still broken -
spittal descending on my face
I watch the young man
destroy my home
cardboard splitting, collapsing
he and his friends move forward
'We don't want maggots like you'
I squirm and try to leave my refuge
'Can't you understand you old cunt
there is a perfectly good river with your name on it... do us all a favour,
Use it.'
I feel the hair on my bowed head pulled.as I am dragged forward
towards the rail.
'Please' I cry, 'don't hurt me.'
'It's an old woman I hear one of them say.'
Hope rises.
'So fucking what' replies my tormentor. 'Vermin's vermin.'
I try to clutch the steel barrier.-arthritic fingers finding no purchase.
Please let someone see me fall.

Nigel Hall

The Man Who Does Magic

Lee opened his eyes and groaned. The strained noise that emerged from somewhere near the back of his throat was similar to the one his mum's old Vauxhall Nova used to make when its choke was being pulled out. He was sure he was about to throw up but thought if he took long deep breaths (*in through the nose, out through the mouth*) whilst also counting down from ten, he might just manage to keep it down. It didn't work and he was sick before he'd even reached seven.

It was dark, deathly dark, and his view was partly obscured by a pair of bulging rhododendron bushes. But from these, the outline of a bench, *and* the iron railings he was propped up against, he worked out he was in a park. How long had he been here, he wondered. Hours? Certainly he couldn't remember *getting* to the park.

I'm never drinking again, he thought, as a memory of a bar lined with Jager bombs flashed into his mind. To try to ease the dull ache at the front of his head, he ripped the Afro wig from his head and hurled it to the rain-sodden ground. The taut elastic had left a raw red ridge around the top of his forehead and he winced when he touched it with his fingertips. However, this was the least of his worries because, when he looked down, he saw he'd been stripped of his fancy dress costume. The only item of clothing his fellow stags had left him (apart from the wig) was his underpants. One of them, Chris he suspected, had used a marker pen to scrawl a large black 'L' on the front of them, though from the angle Lee was looking at it from it looked more like a 'V'.

He started to stand but found his left arm, which had been resting on the railings' cold concrete base, was restricted. He frowned, glanced to it and saw one end of a pair of pink fluffy handcuffs had been fastened snuggly to his wrist. Lee didn't need to look to know the other end had been snagged to the railings. Thanks guys, he thought, although he couldn't help but smile. Surely they'd not left him though, not on his wedding day. He roll-called their names: "Chris, Adam, Pete, very funny. You can come out now."

No answer.

He called again, louder, and this time was rewarded with the sound of slow shuffling footsteps. Moments later a hunched silhouette emerged from the shadows. Lee opened his mouth to jokingly berate his friend but quickly closed it again when he realized *this* shadow belonged to a stranger.

"Can you help me, please?" he asked, embarrassed. He levered his legs to try to hide his bare chest. "My mates have played a bit of a practical joke on me."

The figure, a man's, shuffled closer. "Oh I can see that. You're in a right pickle, aren't you?"

The man's face, lined with deep-set wrinkles, was enshrouded in a thick greasy beard. His clothes – purple shell suit bottoms and a dark navy bomber jacket - were grubby and torn, and he had overly long fingernails, which were thick and gnarled like tree-roots. A tramp, Lee thought. Still, better than nothing.

"Please," he pleaded, "I'm getting married tomorr…*today!* I need to get out of these handcuffs, pronto. Can you get help?"

The man, ignoring Lee's plea, sat down on the bench. Beneath his beard Lee was sure he was smiling. "Married you say. I got married once."

Lee smiled stiffly out of politeness. "Listen mate," he said, more forcefully this time, "I'd love to chat but, as I said, I'm getting married in a few hours and…"

The man cut him off. "She was beautiful. She had skin like porcelain, like a china doll. I used to call her China Doll." The man half-turned and stared pensively off into the distance. "See, she was *from* China and she had skin like a china doll. That's why I called her Ch…"

"Yeah mate, I get it. Now if you could just get someone to help me out of these things, I would *really* appreciate it."

The man acknowledged the handcuffs with a nod. "Do you not have the key? The key would get you out of them things."

Exasperated, Lee pursed his lips, tight like he was sucking through a straw. "No mate. No key." With his free arm he started rubbing at the goose bumps that had appeared along his thighs.

"Your friends do that?" asked the man.

"Yeah."

"Some friends. *Fancy* not leaving a key."

Lee chose to ignore the hint of sarcasm in the man's voice and shouted, "HELP. CAN ANYBODY HEAR ME?"

"No one will come," said the man somewhat astutely. "It'll be another hour at least before people start showing their faces; *at least* another hour."

Could Lee perhaps squeeze his hand out the cuffs? He tucked his thumb tightly into his palm, grasped the one handcuff with his free hand and pulled hard. He'd once watched a police drama where a desperate prisoner had escaped from handcuffs by breaking a thumb. At the time he'd thought it implausible, now he wasn't so sure.

"You got children?" asked the man. He'd pulled a dented tin of tobacco from his bomber jacket pocket and had started to roll a cigarette. Lee let go of the cuffs and shook his head.

"Planning on having any?"

"Not sure." This was a lie. He desperately wanted children and just the thought of it made him giddy with excitement. However, if the man wasn't going to help him he just wanted him to leave. Besides, didn't he have a Big Issue to go and sell?

"I have two," said the man. "A son and a daughter, but we haven't spoken in years."

"Really?" said Lee, and although he wasn't particularly interested, he asked, "Why's that?"

The man's response hit Lee like a juggernaut. "One of them's dead. I last spoke to Sophie when she was four. If she was still alive she'd be thirty-four." His eyes glazed as if replaying a long lost image. "Years, you see," he added.

Snippets of pity stabbed at Lee's conscience. "I'm sorry," he mumbled. "What about your son?"

Although the man had heard, he didn't reply. Instead he pointed to a flowerbed. "What are those?"

"Er, flowers," said Lee sarcastically.

The man rolled his eyes. "I mean, what *kind* of flowers?"

Why's it important, thought Lee. "I don't know," he said curtly.

"Well I'll tell you. Those ones there are Bullseye Geraniums, or *Pelargonium Hortorum*. The red ones are French Marigolds, or *Tagetes Patula*, and the tall ones that have flowers like bells are called…"

"Snapdragons." Lee smiled smugly.

"or…? Now it was the man's turn to smile smugly.

Lee shrugged his shoulders.

"Anthirrhinum Majus."

"You know your flowers," said Lee, impressed.

"I know my park," replied the man.

Lee, conscious that time was ticking away, twisted his neck to peer through the railings behind him. The sky overhead was tinged with red now and he could hear birds beginning to stir.

"The Marigolds were out when she left me," said the man. "We had a whole garden full of them, which means it must have been about this time of year, don't you think?"

Lee frowned. He was about to ask who but then remembered.

"This girl you're going to marry," said the man, "do you love her?"

The question threw Lee and he felt himself blush. "Of course," he said quietly, "otherwise I wouldn't be marrying her, would I?"

"Then you must tell her," said the man, "you must tell her *everyday*. Even if there are days when you don't feel like telling her." He paused and, the next time he spoke, his voice had dissolved into a whisper. "Never stop talking, even if it's to argue. Because, if you can't be bothered even to argue, then you're done for."

Lee, all out of sarcastic comments, simply nodded and muttered "okay." For a long time after that they didn't speak, so Lee filled the awkward silence by repeatedly jiggling the handcuffs.

"What happened?" he asked eventually. "With your wife?"

The man sucked hard on his roll-up and exhaled. The smoke, entwined like a corkscrew to begin with, slowly separated into thin, delicate wisps.

"She left me," he said. "Although to be fair, we'd left each other long before she eventually walked out the door, if you get my meaning."

Lee did.

"I'm sorry," he said. As he watched the tracks of smoke, he felt his fingers start to twitch. "You've not got a spare have you mate?" he asked.

The man grinned mischievously. "Normally it's me asking. I'll roll one for you."

He pulled out his tobacco and papers and rolled one left-handed. Lee looked on, full of admiration. He'd never quite mastered roll-ups and envied those who could do them. Once the man had finished, he handed it to him then made a swift cocking movement with his hand. From behind it, and apparently from thin air, a lighter appeared.

"Magic as well," said Lee.

He placed the roll-up in his mouth and took a long deep drag. The accompanying nicotine rush dulled his pre-wedding jitters slightly and, for a few seconds, the worry of how he was going to free his self of the handcuffs dissipated.

"You're good at roll ups," he commented.

The man nodded knowingly. "I get a lot of practice sitting here. One of my university tutors taught me how to do them."

Lee's eyes widened with surprise. "*You* went to university?" He immediately felt embarrassed. "I'm sorry," he said. "I didn't mean to…"

The man waved a hand dismissively. "You see what everyone else sees, only a tramp. It was another life, but yes, I have a degree and several other pieces of embossed paper with my name on, *some* in swirled lettering. Certainly I'm over qualified for bench sitting, don't you think?"

Lee looked at the man again, this time through less abrasive eyes. He had a sudden urge to peel back the man's beard so he could glimpse more of the person underneath. "Can I ask you a question?" he asked hesitantly.

The man nodded. From the subtle droop of his eyelids he appeared to have guessed what it was going to be.

"How did you end up homeless?"

The man scratched his lips stiffly, as if trying to work out the answer.

"You like noodles?" he asked. He didn't wait for Lee to respond. "*I* like noodles. China Doll and me used to eat them a lot. She'd use chopsticks; I'd use a fork. Noodles are easier to eat with a fork because you can tangle them around the prongs. What you don't want is for those noodles to *un*tangle. If they do that they'll slide off your fork and drop back into the bowl. My life was like those noodles: it untangled. It started with the death of our daughter. Her name was Sophie and she was four. Her little body was broken beyond repair. By a car. The man driving it was drunk, steaming drunk apparently, like I was for ten years afterwards." He sighed and ran a hand down the length of his beard. "I was so wrapped up in my grief for my daughter, I forgot I had a son. By the time I'd sobered up everything I had loved had slid away, like those noodles." He fixed Lee with a stare. "I assume you were drinking tonight."

Lee nodded.

"You drank so much you can't quite fathom out how you ended up here."

Lee nodded again.

"Likewise."

They both sucked their roll-ups and exhaled simultaneously.

"What's your son's name?" asked Lee.

"Arthur."

The man plunged his hand into one of his fraying trouser pockets and pulled out a crumpled scrap of paper. His thick fingers, brown and calloused at the tips, flattened it out gently.

"What you got there?" asked Lee, craning his neck to try to see.

"It's my son's telephone number. I found him in the book some time ago."

"Have you rung it?"

The man 's eyes narrowed. "No," he said quietly.

"Why not?"

"Why do you think?" asked the man.

"How long's it been since you've seen him?" asked Lee.

The man's sigh quivered. "When China Doll left me he was fourteen, which was fourteen years ago. Do you know what the last thing he said to me was? He said, 'I'm sorry, Dad.' Not 'you drunken mess,' or 'sort yourself out,' but 'sorry', like it was *his* fault. He might have been sorry that day but I've been sorry every day since."

He asked Lee, "How old are you, son?" The man's brow furrowed tightly at the word 'son', like it had snuck into the sentence without him realizing.

"Twenty-eight." answered Lee.

"Your dad proud of you?"

Lee shrugged his shoulders and half-smiled. "My dad's dead."

"I'm sorry," said the man.

"It was a while ago. Cancer. Just lately I've been thinking about him a lot though."

Understanding why, the man nodded. "Do you miss him?"

"Every day," replied Lee. "Do you miss your son?"

"Every day," replied the man.

Suddenly, and as if he could no longer bear its taste, the man hurled his roll-up to the floor. He jumped from the bench and walked up to Lee. Lee saw he'd made a fist and, for a moment, was worried, but then the man blew on it and opened out his hand. Dangling from one finger, Lee saw a handcuffed sized key. The man smirked.

"Abracadabra."

"Where did you find that?" asked Lee, relieved.

"It was on the arm of the bench. I found it when I first sat down. Your friends must have left it there so anyone walking past could release you."

Lee's expression hardened. "What! You mean you've had the key all along?"

"Yes," said the man, without the slightest hint of an apology.

Lee, angry now, said, "While I've been sat here freezing my… *I'm getting married in a few hours."*

"I know you are."

"Jeez, why didn't you just give it to me at the start?"

"I'll tell you why. Do you know how long it's been since I've had a conversation with someone? A proper one that doesn't include the words 'spare change.' No? Well I'll tell you. Four months. It's been four months." He sounded bitter, but also terribly sad.

"I sit in the same park every day," he continued. "I see the same faces *every day*. When I sit on this bench next to those same faces, do you know what they do? They get up and walk off. Not straight away, they have *some* manners, but they *do* walk away. Like you would have done if you'd not had them handcuffs on."

The truth forced Lee's expression to soften. The man, feeling guilty himself perhaps, handed over the key.

"They'll be taxis now," he said. "Just head down the street and you'll be able to flag one."

Lee looked despondent. "I've got no money. My wallet was in my trousers. My mates took my trou…"

The man rolled his eyes, delved his hand into his trouser pocket and pulled out some change. "It's all I've got, but it'll do. Ring someone, get 'em to come and pick you up. Failing that, flag a taxi. *Maybe* they'll take pity on you."

"Don't you need the money?" asked Lee.

"Course I bloody do," said the man, "but, at this precise moment, I think you need it more."

Lee nodded his thanks. He took the coins and pressed them in his palm, like they were the most precious things in the world. "What about you?" he asked. "How long are you going to keep your son waiting?"

The man mouthed 'no' and possibly 'it's too late', although beneath that beard it was difficult to tell.

Lee tried again.

"You were right. All I saw was a tramp, but now I see a man, a man who wants to make amends. Your son will see the same, just give him that chance."

The man shook his head. "Got a magic wand 'ave you? Thought not."

Lee was about to extend a hand, to introduce his self properly, but the man walked off.

"My name's Lee," Lee called after him. "What's yours?"

The man didn't reply, and as he faded back into the shadows, Lee saw him drop the scrap of paper on the floor.

*

Lee raced down the street the man had told him he'd find a telephone box on. When he finally spotted one, he ran over to it. Once inside, he lifted the receiver and carefully dialed the number.

"Hello, is that Arthur?" he asked when it was answered. Glancing to the paper in his hand, he smiled. "You don't know me but I'm ringing about your dad."

Daniel Emlyn-Jones

Lily's Grave

Paul slept beside the grave of Lily Conway (1913-1998). The grass was soft there, and at night he was well concealed by the darkness. Many graves in the churchyard were crumbling, crosses swaying in the earth like hands grasping from quicksand, but Lily's was well cared for. On the headstone was written "Beloved Mother and Grandmother", and every week the stone was washed clean, and fresh flowers placed in the flower holder. Lilies they were, to match the name, and Paul fell asleep in their fragrance. Sometimes in the depth of the night, when the noise of the drinkers had faded, and the prowling silhouettes of the dealers had vanished, he would whisper to her, telling her how PJ was hurting his Mum, and from the stillness and the black he imagined an old voice comforting him.

For churchwarden Mrs Phythian-Jones, every morning was a battle against empty beer cans, used needles, used nappies and condoms, and the army of fiends who produced them. The problem had persisted for years, despite endless meetings with the parish council, the city council and the police. Words like "alcoholism", "addiction" and "homelessness" were bandied about. According to the vicar the problem needed "love" and "understanding". As far as she was concerned, the problem needed nothing but a good kick up its backside. The layabouts needed to pull their socks up, sober up, get jobs, and start contributing to society, instead of loafing about in churchyards making nuisances of themselves.

She found a condom lying on a First World War grave, and let out an anguished "well really!", before plucking the offending item from the Portland stone with her litter pick and placing it in the plastic bag. She then found a scrunched can of Special Brew on the grave of the matron of the old workhouse, Maud Heatherton (1807-1888). On the headstone, in large gothic letters peppered with yellow lichen was written: "The Devil finds work for idle hands", and she read the words longingly.

Paul was woken by the clattering of cans. The sun was already high in the sky and he frantically tore himself from his sleeping bag. He was desperately trying to roll it up when a litter pick appeared in his face. He looked up to see an old woman with blue rinse bouffant glowering down at him over half-moon reading spectacles. He had slept late again. She had a shrill posh voice which rent the air like iced needles.

"...buck up your ideas young man...pull your socks up...wrong attitude...contribute to society...holy ground...quiet green space...sacrilege..."

He tried to speak but all he could do was to stutter. He'd always stuttered, but usually got by. Since PJ, the problem had grown so severe he was virtually unable to speak. He grabbed his sleeping bag and rucksack and sprinted towards the churchyard wall, tripping over a headstone in the process.

"And let that be a lesson to you!" she shouted after him.

He slumped against the wall, and as he properly woke up, remembered it was August 15th, his sixteenth birthday, and he wanted to see his Mum. He hadn't seen her for two weeks, since PJ had thrown him out of the flat, beating him so badly that the bruises still hurt. Apart from missing her, begging wasn't getting him much food, and he was famished.

PJ's flat was about seven blocks away, and as Paul got closer to it, he scanned his surroundings nervously. The man had the build of an oversized gorilla, and a unique strut. The flat was on the second floor of a four storey block, and on the other side of the road was an ample privet hedge. Paul carefully edged his way along a wall, doing his best to keep out of the flat's sight line, and then crouched down and manoeuvred himself behind the hedge. He saw PJ's car there, a big flashy blue BMW, and got a sudden urge to grab a rock and scratch the words "EVIL BASTARD" into the paint of the bonnet, but knew he could be seen through the flat's living room window. PJ did a late shift, and usually left the flat by noon, so Paul edged himself into a comfortable position behind the privet and waited. His Mum had raved over PJ's internet profile when she met him online a year before. He was a muscled stubbled stud with a fine arts degree from Loughborough; she was reeling him in and no one was going to stop her. He wasn't just good looks either. He bought her flowers and chocolates, took her out for posh dinners, and told her how beautiful and special she was. She hadn't worn makeup since Paul's Dad left her over a decade before, but suddenly she got a heap of the stuff from Boots and spent hours putting her face on whenever she was due to see him. Paul knew that moving in with him was a bad idea. The man was hiding something, he could see that, but she was too besotted to listen.

The front door opened and a suited PJ emerged and strutted to his car. Paul muffled a gasp with his hand. PJ revved the car as if he were about to compete in the Grand Prix, and then drove off. Paul waited until the car had disappeared around the corner at the end of the street, and then gingerly emerged from the bushes and crossed to the flat. He pressed the intercom button, and when his mum answered, all he could manage was a "Mam mam ma ma ma." There was silence, and then a gasp at the other end. Paul heard the sound of a door opening and closing, and then his Mum came down the stairs to the front door. Paul fell into her arms and started crying. She recoiled slightly, but let him embrace her.

"Where are you staying?" she asked. "The school rung. They say you haven't been attending."

"B-b-b-b-b-b-birth-d-d-d-d-d-d-day," he said.

She nodded, and there was a look of mortification on her face.

"L-l-l-l-l-leave!"

She shook her head. "I can't."

"Wh-wh-wh-wh-wh-wh-why?"

"I just can't. I know it sounds crazy, but….I love him."

The words were like a knife in Paul's heart.

"Wait here." His Mum dashed upstairs and came back with a box of Tesco Bakewell tarts wrapped in a plastic bag. Paul was putting them into his rucksack when a blue BMW purred into the parking space behind him. There was the violent wrench of a handbrake, and then PJ got out.

"I saw you hiding in the bushes you little faggot."

"Let him be. It's his birthday," his mother pleaded.

"Go back upstairs Stella. I'm only telling you once!"

She obeyed immediately.

He turned back to Paul. "It's your birthday is it? Well here's a present for the birthday boy. Perhaps it will teach you to be a man." He hit him round the head and he fell to the ground.

"I warned you not to come back you little pansy. Telling tales to the police, trying to cause trouble between me and my girlfriend? Jealous are you? Wished I'd shacked up with you instead of yer mam do ye?"

"N-n-n-n-n-n-no!" yelled Paul.

"I told you to f-f-fuck off the other week, so why don't you do the f-f-fuck what you're f-f-fucking told!?" He hurled Paul's rucksack into the road.

Paul grabbed it and fled.

Paul sat on a bench outside the churchyard wall until dusk approached, and then lay down in his usual place next to Lily's grave. He was aching all over, and when he looked at his fading reflection in the shining granite of Lily's headstone, he saw that he had a big black eye. Once darkness had fallen, he carefully unpacked the box of Bakewell tarts, and steadily munched his way through them. He left half a piece uneaten, and placed it on Lily's grave. As he lay there, the stars remote above the yellow pall of the city, he decided that one way or another, the following day, he'd take his own life.

"I've warned you before, and this time I'm calling the police!"

Paul let out a moan as he was prodded with the litter pick. He rolled in his sleeping bag to get away from the object, and banged his head on a nearby headstone. He was disorientated and dizzy as he clambered out of the sleeping bag and tried to make for the churchyard wall. He ran headlong into a man, and then fell to the ground.

"It's alright, I'll deal with this," the man said to the old woman.

"No, I am dealing with this! I'll tell you what I'm going to do. I'm going right back into that church, and I'm going to call the police from the sacristy telephone. I've had enough of my churchyard being treated like a doss house."

"For God's sake woman, can't you see the poor lad's injured?"

The old woman looked at Paul and hesitated. "Oh very well, you deal with it if you must, but this is a churchyard, and we simply can't accommodate everyone who wants to sleep here. It isn't appropriate." She walked off, swinging her litter pick as if it were a Kalashnikov.

The man helped Paul up, and put a hand on his shoulder. Paul flinched away.

"I'm not going to hurt you," he said. "How long have you been sleeping here?"

"Two-two-two-two-two-two-two-weeks."

"OK. Well how about I buy you some breakfast?"

Paul nodded. The man's eyes were kind, and in his hand was a bouquet of lilies.

"I just need to see to my grandmother's grave, and then we can go to the café over the way." He knelt down at Lily's grave and arranged the flowers in the flower holder in front of the headstone. He then filled a bucket and gave the granite a wash.

"She was a very special woman," he said.

Paul knew this already, though he didn't know how.

In a nearby café Paul devoured a full English breakfast, a heap of toast, butter and marmalade, and several cups of coffee. He could have eaten the same again, but didn't like to ask.

"So, in your own time, can you tell me what's been happening, and maybe I can help."

Paul tried speaking, but the stuttering was so bad he couldn't even form a word. He tried several times, and then began to cry.

The man put a hand on his shoulder. "Now listen. I'm here to help you. I promise I'm not going to hurt you. Speak slowly, as slowly as you like."

Paul looked into the man's eyes. Tears glistened there. He took a deep breath, and then syllable by syllable, word by word, he told the man his story.

Tom Mooney

The Invisibles

This town, like any town, looks different through different sets of eyes. The locals see the SALE signs in giant shop windows, the lines of cars and lorries blocking their paths to work on the one-way system, the smog breath of exhaust pipes. Visitors see the intricate carvings on the corners of the old buildings near the corn exchange, the restaurants, Thai and Moroccan and Indian and Lebanese and good old fish 'n' chips. The race-goers, on days like this, see gushing tsunamis of watered-down Guinness, buses and train timetables, discarded Racing Posts and little blue pens and losers' betting slips.

Few of them see me. I am the invisible, intolerable, inexplicable face of every town. Nearby pigeons shock when I stir in doorways or on benches, so oblivious even are they to my presence. Just how I like it.

But tonight I walk the streets. I make myself visible for these four days every year, *make* them see me. The race-goers. The tweed-clad, drunken Daves, day off work for a piss-up and a gamble, maybe buy a new hat if a couple of nags come in, check out the small-town snatch in Flares later on, the wife'll never find out. You know the types. One thing they have got this time of year – full pockets and enough of the black stuff in them to share it. Whether it is sheer drunkenness or a buried guilt of some sort floating to the surface, they are more inclined to chuck a note than a punch.

Not that it don't come without its dangers, mind. This week aint for everyone. Some of the community (ha!) wouldn't dare set foot in town tonight. They're all camped out in the bitter field, or under the blue bridge, or there's bound to be a few in the bushes by the cycle track. They don't like the risks involved. More pissed wankers = more chances a pissed wanker will have a pop. But old timers like me, veterans of the streets, we know this is the time to make hay and we know how to do it. Festival week comes but once a year. The young 'uns – and the old-but-new 'uns – they'll learn. I get it. I was in their sleeping bags once. Most won't last a year at this life. That's not a snobbish criticism, it's a fact. Whatever it is they ran away from will call them back. Warm beds and mum's cottage pie. Kids. Girlfriends or jobs or dealing. Good luck to them. A few will stay, endure, learn to live this life. Because that's what it is. Life. It doesn't take place in a three-bedroom semi. There's no company share scheme. No suit and tie, unless you get bloody unlucky at the clothes bank. It's just a way of life when it's all boiled down, a choice. Not a first choice, admittedly, but a choice. We, I, have chosen this life. Chosen life. Chosen over sorting out whatever shit we had going on before we ended up on the streets. Chosen over throwing ourselves into the icy November river.

I'm in Boots tonight. I was surprised when I got here that it wasn't already taken. The cold's probably kept a few of them away. Boots – fair play to them – have shutters only on the doors, leaving a cosy 4ft x 6ft cave, ripe for a few hours of speculation. It's a nice walk up, even this week if you get your timing right. Up from the river across the cobbled bit of town, step-for-step with the ghosts of a century's drinkers and market traders and tourists. The church spire peers over the rows of shops, keeping an eye on how the evening's progressing.

I've got my extra thick coat on, to counter the mid-March chill. Not a bad bit of kit, picked it up a year or so ago from the clothes bank. Reckon it's good for a couple of winters if I look after it right. I wash it in the laundrette pretty regular to keep it looking nice. Only ever on Tuesday's, mind, when Karen's working there on her own. She lets me use the washers and dryers for free if I stay out the back away from the other customers. Nice girl, she is. See, it is all about who you know in this town. Karen used to volunteer at the centre but doesn't have the time any more. Now she helps us out with clothes washing, like she's started her own little charity.

It's getting busier now, people swaying over the cobbles, in and out of wine bars and little pubs with the footy on. 1-0 Arsenal, last I saw. I spied it as I walked past the window – I know, I know, I broke one of the golden rules. Rule 37(b); Homeless people should walk only with their heads lowered, never risking eye contact with the Normal People.

I've got my hat laid flat out in front of me to catch the pieces of silver and paper dropped in my direction and my hair's looking wild and unkempt. Which it is. No other equipment nowadays, no props. I've tried it all. When I first graduated from homeless to homeless beggar – a difficult mental adjustment – I kept it simple. Just a sad face and a cupped hand. But no-one wants to go near the depressed, the crazy. Then I tried music but I never was the most talented with an instrument. I was thrown out of the choir at junior school because I couldn't sing. What the hell does that teach kids about the inclusiveness of society? Perhaps I should have seen it as an omen. Anyway, I saved up for a couple of days and bought a ukulele from the charity shop, only a tenner. I thought it would be easy to learn and I aint exactly pressed for rehearsal time. But it was so damn difficult I gave up after a week. I tried a dog once, too. A little Jack Russell stray I picked up. But that only meant old ladies and sympathetic dog owners bought pasties from Greggs for the bloody mutt, leaving less in their hearts for me. Little bastard ran off just as I was warming to him. Now though, it's just me and the hat. I try to look at least a little respectable, so no-one's scared to approach. And not look too depressed. That happy (non-singing, non-dog-owning) tramp look, you know?

Groups of lads stride up and down, the cacophony of their echoey banter bouncing off the old shop walls. Hysterical giggles and in-jokes and rugby tackles. In a big group at least one lad will stop and drop. Usually with a sympathetic face. Or someone will chuck in a tenner and tell me he's "had a good day, if you know what I mean mate". Yeah I know what you mean big fella, ta very much, enjoy your hangover.

All pretty standard, no nastiness about, despite the violent, thick edge to the air you always get on Saturday nights. The key is to get what you came for and leave before the top shelf spirits start seeping into the bloodstream. Before the Red Bull fuels the fire inside them, makes them invincible, makes them *really* see me. But there's a lad making a beeline for me and he aint dressed like the rest. No pinstripe, no flat cap, no brogues. He's big, fat and round and he's wearing a tight morph suit with a Welsh flag emblazoned on it. A matching coloured wig completes this cat's look.

"Alright mate," he says to me, all sullen, offering a tired half-smile and gesturing that he wants to sit down. I don't see anyone else with him so, after studying the odds, I nod yeah and he enters my cave. "I'm Craig," he offers.

"Jim," I lie.

"Well, nice to meet you Jim old boy."

There's a long silence, minutes maybe, which unnerves me. This kid's barely 25 and he's got the forlorn look of a man twice his age. He stares soullessly at the passing night, sighing bitterly at the revellers who pass by, taking little notice of their jibes. I don't like this one bit. I hate conversations with pissed people. It rarely ends well, occasionally disastrously. But his sorrow makes me feel compelled to break our deadlock.

"What is it then, stag do?" I say, nodding at his outfit.

"Yeah, yeah. Had enough already though."

"Oh. Doubts or something is it?"

He chuckles. "No, no, not that. It's just I realised tonight I may well fucking hate every one of my friends. If I can still call them that."

"Ah," I say, considering my next words carefully. "We all get to that stage, my friend. How do you think I ended up here?"

He mulls this statement over, tasting every layer of its bitter flavour, before deciding it deserves a smile. Up he gets and he's offering me his hand, a gesture I always pretend I don't see. But I shake it loosely because I can see he needs it.

"Thank you, Jim," he says. "You are one fucking wise man. Have a good night, sir." And with that he spins and stumbles back to Wetherspoons, where I hear his friends asking what the fuck he was doing sitting in a doorway with a tramp/gyppo/scab (delete as appropriate).

With that I decide to go. The stench of whiskey he left in the cave signals silly season is about to start. I collect my things; hat, coat, sleeping bag, today's newspaper, the cash and coins from tonight's takings, of course. And I'm gone, moving swiftly over the cobbles. Ghosting through the dim streetlight like a ninja, away from the din of town. The town that in a few hours, after barely an hour's sleep, will breathe back into life. The promise of street cleaners sweeping away the night, butchers dressing windows, commuters battling for seats on the bus. The smells of the ale and sweat and fried chicken replaced by fry-ups and pollution and crisp dewy grass. But on I go. Past the rowdy queue out the door of Subway, past the wine-bar bouncers all suited up for action, past the eerie church gates and out towards the cycle track, the deserted haven of The Invisibles.

Gary Bowness

Room Thirty Four

A single act play.

Synopsis: Room Thirty Four.

In August 2014, Eighteen-year-old Chris Williams makes himself homeless to escape his mother's abusive boyfriend, Billy Newton and his criminal associates in Newcastle's West End. Fleeing in the early hours gives Chris a head start but with little money and no plan he travels to Sunderland. A devastating rejection by Sunderland Council's Homeless Team forces Chris back to Newcastle and into Collingwood House, a city centre homeless accommodation. There, he meets Marty, a streetwise Glaswegian, who, after serving a prison sentence for violence found Collingwood whilst being street homeless. Marty enlightens Chris to hostel realities but with Marty set to move on, Chris must learn fast. When Marty is out, Chris's unsavoury neighbour, Ash, entertains a visitor, Glen Watson, Billy Newton's cousin. Watson is a merciless thug who harbours criminal aspirations for Collingwood House out of room thirty four. Hiding behind room thirty four's locked door, Chris, the unknown new boy, contemplates the dilemma of becoming street homeless or police informing. In a rational moment, Chris devises a plan and Watson and his Collingwood House associates are arrested. Chris finally has his second chance but with it the uncertainty of how long that might last.

Characters

CHRIS Anxious, away from home for the first time. Eighteen years old.
MARTY Independent and caring. Twenty one years old.

Setting

Newcastle Upon Tyne in the NE1 postcode area.

Time

August 2014

Act 1

Late afternoon in room thirty four, Collingwood House, a homeless hostel.

Collingwood House is a hostel for sixteen to twenty-five year-old homeless people. It has fifty rooms. Each room has a single bed, a table and chair. Between the table and chair and the bed is a walk space. At the end of the table, towards the foot of the bed there's a small wardrobe. The room's door is situated behind the bed and leads into a communal corridor. In room thirty four, CHRIS is going through a holdall when there's a knock at the door. He shoves the holdall right under the bed, creeps to the door and looks through the spy-hole.

Chris: Who is it?
Marty: Alright mate? It's Marty from next door.
(Pause.)
Chris: What do you want?
Marty: I've got some footie mags for you.
(Long Pause)
I'll leave them outside your door.
Chris: No, wait there.
He opens the door.
Come in.
Marty places the bag on the table.
Marty: It's Chris isn't it?
Chris: Yeah.
Marty: I'm Marty.
Marty offers his hand, they shake.
Chris: Alright Marty.
(Pause.)
Marty: Can I sit down?
Chris: Er. . . yeah.
Marty sits on the bed as Chris rests against the table.
Marty: There's some fresh pasties in there as well.
Chris: Thanks.
Marty: You don't have to eat them but I heard that you moved in with nothing.
Chris: Who said?
Marty: I overheard the staff downstairs.
(Pause.)
Chris: What else did they say?

Marty: Nothing that's all I heard. Anyway, I went to the Peoples' Kitchens.

(Pause.)

Have you ever been?

Chris: No.

Marty: I'll take you tomorrow.

(Pause.)

Or I can bring stuff back. They've got sandwiches, soup, sausage rolls…

Chris: Yeah, just whatever. What's it like in here?

Marty: Alreet if you keep yer head down.

Chris: What do you mean?

Marty: Did-ne grass, did-ne get into cliques. Just do your own thing.

Chris: Cliques?

Marty: Aye. Like sitting in groups and chasing the dragon till three in the morning.

Chris: I don't like stuff like that.

Marty: Some do though and they'll want ta cadge off yer.

Chris: I've nothing to cadge.

Marty: And they'll try'n sell yer stuff.

Chris: Not interested.

Marty: Show them nothing and they'll not rob yer.

Chris: In this corridor?

Marty (head gesture): Nah, the next cluster along.

Chris: Who?

Marty: Ash and her mates.

Chris sits beside Marty.

Chris: Ash?

Marty: On tag after getting outta jail: street robberies to buy smack.

Chris: A lass doing robberies?

Marty: Aye but she fights like a lad.

(Pause.)

And her lad, Ant's a dealer.

Chris: And they let him in here?

Marty: As a visitor. They knocked his application back. Wideboy, as nice as pie to them downstairs to keep everything sweet.

Chris: Do the staff know he deals?

Marty: They're not stupid but they can-ne prove anything.

Chris: What's he like?

Marty: Horrible basta, keep yer door locked all the time.

Chris: When's he in?

Marty: Six til nine and sometimes sleeps over.

Chris: What does he look like?
Marty: Big, tattoos on his neck, brown hair. You'll know him when you see him.
(Pause.)
Chris: What's this cluster like?
Marty: Sound. I'm next to you. Opposite me, Adam, he's at college doin 'A' Levels. Good lad; likes the kitchen kept tidy.
Chris: I'm tidy anyway.
(Pause.)
'A' Levels?
Marty: Aye. Maths and others. He's applied to uni. He's around at night: has his scran, plays pool in the common room then gets his head down.
(Pause.)
Oh aye, next to you there's Ali. Keeps himself to himself. He escaped from Iraq.
Chris: Escaped from Iraq?
Marty: Aye, from all the killing, sixteen and on his own. Escaped though Turkey and across Europe but he never talks about it. You hardly see him; goes to the Kurdish Centre.
Chris: Does he speak English?
Marty: Better than me but that does-ne say much.
(Pause.)
Chris: Who was in here?
(Pause.)
Marty (breaks eye contact:) Michelle.
Chris: What's wrong?
(Pause)
Marty: She was about to move in with her boyfriend and he dumped her so she came back. Wee Rachel wanted to borrow a lighter and got no answer. Her door was locked so Rachel called the staff. They got there just in time; she'd tried to hang herself from the shower.
Chris (looks towards the ensuite, shocked:) What?
Marty: Aye. Never be as lucky again.
(Pause.)
Marty (cont:) That's history, she's moved on, living with her Gran now.
(Pause)
Chris: What about the others?
Marty: Keep away from Maccam Steve. Gobshite, he's serious bother.
Chris: Maccam Steve?

Marty: You can-ne miss him; he never takes his Sunderland top off. He's even worn it at the back gate on a match day to wind Newcastle fans up.

Chris: Tss! Lucky they didn't smash this place up.

Marty: Nearly took the gate off, idiot. Swerve him.

(Pause.)

Oh and dodge Anders and Sparksy. They're Ant's mates. They sign him in when Ash has visitor bans. They're real trouble, nicked all sorts outta rooms.

Chris: Have they been in jail?

Marty: Yeah, burglary.

(Pause.)

Chris: They'll be at home here.

Marty: What do you mean?

Chris: It's like a nick: cameras everywhere, street robbers, dealers and burglars. More criminals in here than in Durham jail.

(Pause.)

Do you keep out of their way?

Marty: No.

Chris: Ever had any trouble?

Marty: No. I'm nee threat to them but they know I won't take any shite either.

Chris: Did anybody ask why you're here? Being Scottish, I mean?

Marty: Some did and I told them.

(Pause.)

I'm not proud but I'm not ashamed either.

(Pause.)

Chris (uneasily): Ashamed?

Marty: Aye. I went home one night an reet before my eyes my mother was on the kitchen floor, seven bells knocked outta her: face covered in blood, pleading with my stepfather not to hit her so I decked the basta.

Chris: Nothing to be ashamed of.

Marty: Aye but when I was getting a tea-towel to clean her up, he came at me, fists fleein. I got the knife off the draining board and stabbed him twice in the guts, he collapsed then I realised what I'd done. My mother went hysterical. I thought I'd killed him.

Chris: What happened?

Marty: Got three years, knocked down to eighteen months on appeal. Got out, ended up in a Probation hostel in Glasgow. Hated it. You think this place is bad.

(Pause)

So I came down here; slept rough for weeks in parks, old buildings, under bridges, anywhere. Then got to know people; met a lass and then went to the council and told them we were living with her mother and that I couldn't stay there anymore.

Chris: Then what happened?

Marty: The Homeless Team contacted these.

Chris: Where's your lass now?

Marty: At her mam's.

Chris: Living there?

Marty: Aye, she's bidding on houses: two bedrooms so there's nee bedroom tax to pay or we'd end up on streets again.

Chris: Bedroom tax?

Marty: Aye. If you've got a spare room yer can-ne get full Housing Benefit so you have to pay some of it; even more if yer get a furniture package from the housing association. We've a bairn on the way so we're alreet, he'll be in the second room.

(Pause.)

Chris: Are you bidding?

Marty: Nee chance. They would-nee give a violent Glaswegian anything, even if he was defending his mother.

Chris: Oh.

Marty: I'll just move in.

(Pause.)

Chris: Have you been in trouble before?

Marty: No. I was a landscaper. I loved it.

Chris: In Scotland?

Marty: Aye, Glasgow. I saw parts that I'd only heard about.

(Pause)

Thorntonhall. I thought I'll live here one day.

(Pause.)

But I got jailed, lost my job, came out, had nowt.

(Pause.)

What about you?

(Pause.)

Och, you're alreet if you did-ne want to say.

Chris: I erm . . . ran away.

Marty: From home?

Chris: Yeah.

Marty: In Newcastle?

Chris: Hmmm.

Marty: You did-ne run far.

Chris (defensively:) I went to Sunderland but the council said I'd made myself homeless and wasn't from Sunderland so they couldn't help.

Marty: When did yer do a runner?

Chris: Today.

Marty: How old are you?

Chris: Eighteen.

Marty: You're alreet, the polis won't be looking.

(Pause.)

Chris: My mother's boyfriend and his mates will be looking for me, not the cops.

Marty: Why?

Chris: Billy, that's my mother's boyfriend wanted me to give a statement to the police saying that his cousin, Glen was with me on the X box last Friday night. He kept asking questions like a copper and hit me when I got things wrong.

Marty: What did yer mother say?

Chris: Nothing.

(Pause.)

She's not bothered. I've even slept in the shed before to get away from them.

(Pause.)

Marty: Christ, man that's worse than being homeless.

Chris: When I left, for the first time since my dad died, I felt free.

(Pause.)

I'd rather be dead than go back there.

Marty: Why a statement?

Chris: Dunno. He wouldn't tell me. Just said if you screw up when they pull our Glen, they'll drag you out of the Tyne.

Marty: Reet hard man eh?

Chris: I agreed just to keep them off my back but then I couldn't sleep thinking about it. Every car that came near, I thought it's the police. Then I thought they'll stitch me up and I'll go down.

(Pause.)

Just before four this morning, I got some clothes and stuff and sneaked out. I prayed the coppers wouldn't stop me. I got to an old cemetery and hid there until a few cars were on the road and then I walked to the Metro.

Marty: Do you know anybody in here?

Chris: No. I looked at office board when Andy was phoning benefits.

Marty: Did you tell Andy?

Chris: No. I said I've had no contact with my family and I've stayed on mate's sofas. But I said if anybody rings to say I'm not here.

Marty: What did he say?

Chris: He agreed and said he'd let the staff know.

Marty: Good.

(Pause.)

Are you okay about going out?

Chris: No.

Marty: I'll bring yer stuff in.

Chris: Cheers Marty.

Marty: What benefits are you on?

Chris: Applied for JSA today with the staff.

Marty: Thing is, you'll have the bullshit job search appointments. They'll tell you how many jobs to apply for every week and if you don't or if you miss appointments, they'll sanction yer benefits.

Chris: They mentioned that so I asked for first thing appointments because them bastards are in bed til dinner time.

Marty: What did they say?

Chris: They couldn't promise anything.

(Pause.)

Have you been sanctioned?

Marty: Aye, when Kerry was ill. I cud-ne leave her spewing in the house, so I waited for her mam to come home. I cud-ne ring them, I had nee credits on my mobile. I ran there but I was half an hour late; they would-nee see me. The only thing this JSA jobs-worth basta said was: appointments are organised to help me find work.

Chris: Did you tell them about Kerry?

Marty: It does-ne mean anything to them. I said what would you have done if you were me? She just said it's not about me Mr. McConnell. I wanted to say did-ne be condescending, you might sit here one day but then thought, you can-ne reason with them so just play the game.

Chris: Are you getting money now?

Marty: Oh Aye that was months ago.

Chris: How long was your sanction?

Marty: Three weeks.

Chris: Three weeks! How did you live?

Marty: Foodbank and Collingwood's welfare fund. When I went back they said next time it could be six months.

Chris: Six months!

Marty: Aye, be very careful, they'll wreck life.

(Pause.)

I've got soup if you want it?

Chris: Thanks Marty, when the staff sort something out, I'll give you some back.

Marty: You're okay.

Marty leaves and comes back with another bag and a cup. He puts them on the table.

Marty: Sorry about the Rangers cup.

Chris: Cheers Marty.

Marty: Nee bother. You'll be like a dog at broth with this lot. There's a wee pan and a dodgy tin opener in there but did-ne leave anything in the kitchen.

Chris: No chance.

Marty: I'm away up to Kerry's, so I'll see yer termorra.

Chris: See you tomorrow.

Marty: Remember to lock your door, Chris.

Chris locks the door and lies on the bed with a magazine. He begins to read and then falls asleep. The stage lights dim and brighten. Loud voices in the corridor awaken him. Disoriented, he sits up.

Offstage

Ash: See that new lad.

Ant: In thirty four?

Ash: Yeah.

A cluster door slams open. There's a knock on the door, the handle turns and the door rattles.

Ant: Are you in?

A bang on the door.

(Pause.)

Ant: Bastards not in!

Ash: Try later!

The cluster door slams closed again. Chris lays motionless. The intercom buzzes, startling him. It stops. He unplugs it, creeps to the door and listens.

Offstage

Ash: Sparksy, here.

Sparksy: What?

The voices become muffled. Chris presses his head against the door. Silence. He paces the room and then sits on his bed. He gets up again and goes back to the door and looks through the spy-hole.

Offstage

Ash: Come to mine when you're done! Where's Anders?

Sparksy: He's coming in a bit.

Muffled banging music is heard. It stops. Silence. The cluster door bangs open, hitting the wall, Chris jumps back. His door bangs again; the handle's tried. The door shakes.
Offstage

Ash: He's not in, Glen, Ant's just been!

Glen: Get to yer door!

Chris darts beside the wardrobe, knocking it.

Ash: He's not in!

Glen: He is I heard something. That bastard's got my room. I've had my name down for ages to get in here!

Ash: Glen, you're on camera!

Glen (Through the door:) When I get my hands on yer I'm going rip yer head off!

Ash: Haway back in here!

Glen: What's his name?

Ash: Dunno. Just see the divvy later.

Glen: Ask them if they know him.

Ash: I'll sort it later!

Glen: I'll take this door off!

The door rattles again

Ash: He's not in!

Glen: He is! Ring him.

Ash: I'll blag the staff later.

Glen: Where's he from?

Ash: I don't know, haway back in here! We'll sort that later.

(Long pause.)

Glen: Got any skins Ash?

Ash: Sparksy's brought some.

Glen: Nice one.

The cluster door bangs closed. Chris waits behind the wardrobe and then crawls to the bed. He drags the holdall out, puts on his jacket, throws the holdall over his shoulder and stops.

(Long pause.)

He puts the hold on the bed, plugs the intercom in and dials.

(Pause.)

Chris: Hello is that Andy?

(Pause.)

Chris (whispering:) It's Chris. Andy, Glen Watson from Elswick's in here. The police are looking for him.

(Pause.)

Don't know but it's serious.

(Pause.)

Andy, can you rub my name off the office board?
(Pause.)
They're sending someone down to check the board. Take my name off.
(Pause)
Call the police.
(Long pause.)
So you'll buzz, hang up and then buzz again when it's okay.
(Pause.)
No, I won't answer the door to anyone.
(Pause.)
Please Don't be long.

Chris sits beside the intercom and then he goes to the door and listens. He paces the room several times and goes back to the intercom. Agitated, he repeats the ritual several times.

Chris: Come on! Come on!

His pace quickens. He stops.

Boots pass Chris's door. He runs to the spy-hole. Everything goes quiet until a loud disturbance erupts.

Offstage.

Ash: Get off them you bastards! They haven't done anything!

Thumping boots and rustling jackets pass Chris's door.

Ash: Get off! Arghh! Get off!

Distant slamming doors and muffled shouting are heard and then silence. Chris goes to the intercom. The stage light dims and brightens. The intercom buzzes, stops and then buzzes again. Chris grabs it.

Chris: Hello!
(Pause.)
It's safe. What happened?
(Pause.)
I understand you can't tell me.
(Pause.)
Chris (cont:) And Watson?
(Long Pause.)
Gone! Great! Thanks Andy!
(Pause.)
Would you keep my name off just for a few days?
(Pause.)
I'm okay.
(Pause.)
Can I talk to you about it tomorrow? I'm not up to it now.
(Pause.)

Thanks Andy. Bye.
Chris (punches the air:) You don't need to worry about this room now Watson, they'll make sure you get one.
He gets the food and heads for the kitchen, whistling The Blaydon Races.
Curtain

Alice Mapplebeck

Soulfest

Scene 1

The street.

Danny is sat down begging from passers-by.

Danny: Could you spare me some change please? Beautiful lady could you spare me some change? Excuse me mate, have you got any change? No? No.

Enter Sadie speaking to offstage.

Sadie: I'll be back soon, just going to give these out. Won't be long.

Danny: Excuse me?

Sadie: Yes?

Danny: Could you spare some change please?

Sadie: No sorry, I don't have any money, but have this.

She hands him a cup.

Danny: What is it?

Sadie: Coffee.

Danny: Thanks.

Sadie: Would you like a biscuit?

Danny: Haven't you got any bacon butties?

Sadie: No sorry, but I can ask someone to go and get you one.

Danny: No it's ok. What you got?

Sadie: Bourbons.

Danny: Urgh, haven't you got any custard creams?

Sadie: No.

Danny: Fine I'll have a bourbon.

Sadie hands Danny the packet.

Danny: Ta.

Beat.

Danny: So, why are you giving away free coffee and biscuits?

Sadie: Its part of a student mission called 'Soul Fest'.

Danny: What's that?

Sadie: It's an outreach programme, where a group of students come together for a week, to make a difference in the community.

Danny: So you're pretty much just giving out free drinks out all the time?

Sadie: We'll be doing other stuff as well.

Danny: Like what?

Sadie: Talking to members of the public, giving out free food.

Danny: Cool.

Sadie: Would you like anything else?

Danny: No thanks.

Pause.

Danny: So when did this mission thing start?

Sadie: Last night.

Danny: Do you like it so far?

Sadie: It's ok.

Danny: So what do they call you?

Sadie: Sadie.

Danny: Danny.

Beat.

Danny: I take it you're a student?

Sadie: Yes. I'm at Liverpool.

Danny: Liverpool?

Sadie nods.

Danny: You from there?

Sadie: No I'm from around here.

Danny: Why did you want to study over there?

Sadie: It's very vibrant and cultural. I just fell in love with the place as soon as I went over. Plus I was getting annoyed with living at home.

Danny looks at Sadie.

Sadie: What?

Danny: You look like a Sadie I once knew.

Sadie: Really?

Danny: Yeah.

Sadie: Well, it won't be me.

Danny: Oh really?

Sadie: Excuse me?

Danny: Oh come on, you don't remember me?

Sadie: No.

Danny: Why not have a closer look.

Sadie: No it's ok.

Danny: I think you should.

Sadie: Fine then.

Sadie does so.

Sadie: *(Gasps)* Danny.

Danny: Yeah.

Sadie: But how…why?

Danny: It's a long story. I can tell you it, if you like?

Sadie: Erm…actually I've just realised I've got to dash.

Danny: Would appreciate it if you stayed.

Sadie: No, I'll see you another time. Bye.

Danny: What about your biscuits?

Sadie: You keep them.

Danny: Will I see you again?

Sadie exits.

Exeunt.

Scene 2

Six years previously.

Danny and Sadie are skimming pebbles across a river.

Danny: Bet you can't do this.

Sadie: Bet I can.

Both compete to see who can make the longest skim. Sadie eventually wins.

Sadie: Yes!

Danny: How did you do that?

Sadie: It's easy.

Danny: But you said you'd never done it before.

Sadie: When did I say that?

Danny: Before when we were walking down. You said:-

Sadie: My Dad taught me when I was little.

Danny: Really?

Sadie: Yeah.

Danny: Can you do anything else?

Sadie: Like what?

Danny: Well…can you touch your nose with your tongue?

Sadie does so followed by Danny.

Danny: Lick your elbow?

Sadie does so. Danny struggles.

Danny: You're…amazing.

Sadie giggles.

Danny pulls out a packet of strawberry laces from his pocket.

Danny: Want one?

Sadie: Please.

They both take a lace.

Danny: Want to see who can eat theirs the fastest?

Sadie: Yeah.

Danny: Ready? One…two…three.

Both race to eat their laces with Danny eventually winning.

Danny: Yes!

Sadie: You cheated.

Danny: Did not.

Sadie: Did too.

Danny: Want to do it again?

Sadie: Yeah.

Danny grabs a lace.

Danny: How about we share it?

Sadie: Ok.

Both grab an end.

Danny: Ready?

Exeunt.

Scene 3

Present day.

The following afternoon.

Danny is sat on the same street corner begging.

Enter Sadie carrying a paper bag containing a hot sandwich.

Sadie: Hello.

Danny: So you're talking to me now?

Sadie: Excuse me?

Danny: I saw you this morning, tried getting your attention, but you ignored me.

Sadie: I didn't even see you. Besides I was probably chatting to the others in my team.

Danny: Fair enough. What you doing now?

Sadie: I came to apologise after running off yesterday, and to make up I've bought you this.

Hands bag to Danny.

Danny: A bacon butty.

Sadie: I know how much you like them.

Danny: Where's it from?

Sadie: Greggs.

Danny: Thanks.

Danny opens out the sandwich, pulls out the bacon and chucks the bread away. Then eats the bacon.

Sadie: What did you do that for?

Danny: Their bread is crap.

Sadie: It's only bread.

Danny: You can go somewhere better next time.

Sadie: No.

Danny: No?

Sadie: I'm not taking orders from you.

Danny: Oh?

Sadie: You're fussy for starters.

Danny: I'm not fussy.

Sadie: Well it's either that or…you know.

Danny laughs.

Sadie: What's so funny?

Danny: You think I'm on crack.

Sadie: Are you?

Danny: Are you?

Short pause.

Danny: No comment.

Sadie: Anyway, I just wanted to give you a sandwich, which you've ruined.

Danny: Fine, if it means that much to you I'll go and eat the bread.

Danny makes a move to stand.

Sadie stops him.

Sadie: No, no, no it's ok. Right I must be going. See you around.

Sadie makes a move to go.

Danny: Sadie wait.

Sadie: Yes?

Danny: Why don't you take a pew?

Sadie: No thanks.

Danny: Are you in a rush somewhere?

Sadie: That's none of your business.

Danny: Well why don't you sit down?

Sadie hesitates.

Sadie: Here?

Danny: It's only the pavement.

Sadie looks around.

Danny: Sadie I'm not going to bite.

Sadie sits down next to Danny.

Danny: What you been up to today?

Sadie: Litter picking.

Danny: Litter picking?

Sadie nods.

Danny: Why were you doing that shit job?

Sadie: It's part of the mission.

Danny: So you're happy doing all the crap that nobody else can be arsed to do?

Sadie: It's the council that normally does that job.

Danny: Yeah but at least they get paid for all that. Honestly I'm surprised at you Sadie.

Sadie: What do you mean?

Danny: You were this incredibly bright and beautiful girl at school who stood up for what she believed in. Now here you are litter picking and giving out drinks to strangers.

Sadie: It only lasts for 10 days.

Danny: Then what will you do afterwards, go and ignore those whom you 'serviced'.

Sadie: Huh?

Danny: Well that's what they all did last year.

Sadie: What do you mean?

Danny: There were loads of students in town last year, offering free food, while providing us with some entertainment from the church. As soon as it was over, they would walk past you without a glance.

Sadie: It was probably your imagination.

Danny: Probably my imagination?

Sadie: I'm sure nobody would just ignore you deliberately.

Danny: You don't believe me do you?

Sadie: Of course not.

Danny: I got to know these two guys quite well. They gave me coffee and we spent ages discussing video games and music. It turned out we had a lot in common. Anyway a week after it was over, I was sat here when I spotted them. I shouted, but they just looked at me blankly and carried on.

Sadie: Gosh, I'm sorry.

Danny: If you think this mission will benefit everyone, then you're naïve.

Sadie: I'm not naïve. Some people did actually benefit from last year's mission.

Danny: Who?

Sadie: Our co-ordinator mentioned this guy, whose life transformed just because of last year.

Danny: Anybody else?

Sadie: Erm…oh just shut up.

Danny: My mates noticed these students happily talked to them one week, but looked down their noses the next.

Sadie: Well my friends said the homeless were quite rude.

Danny: We're not rude.

Sadie: You've no idea how much money and hard work goes into making this a success.

Danny laughs.

Sadie rises.

Sadie: I'm going.

Danny: Oh come one.

Sadie: If you're going to keep acting like this, then you can just sod off!

Danny: Sadie wait.

Sadie: No!

Danny: Fine bitch, be that way!

Sadie exits.

Exeunt.

Scene 4

Six years previously.

Danny is sat outside the head teacher's office.

Enter Sadie.

Sadie: Danny.

Danny looks up at Sadie then looks away.

Sadie: What are you doing here?

Danny: Got sent here by Mr. Butcher.

Sadie: Why?

Danny: I told him where to go.

Sadie: You what?

Danny: He was being a twat.

Sadie: Danny, why?

Danny: I didn't do my homework.

Sadie: Isn't this the second time this week?

Danny: I don't know.

Sadie: Why aren't you doing any?

Danny: I can't.

Sadie: I can help you if you like?

Danny: No.

Sadie: Why didn't you ask a teacher? They won't bite.

Danny: It's easy for you to say isn't it? The bright and popular teacher's pet.

Sadie: Danny.

Danny: You always get A*, the gold merits:-

Sadie: You think it's easy for me, don't you. You don't realise how much effort I put in just to please everybody, especially my parents.

Pause.

Danny: Sorry.

Sadie: Shall I see you by the gates?

Danny: Yeah I'll see you there.

Sadie: Ok. Bye.

Danny: Bye.

Sadie exits.

Exeunt.

Scene 5

Present day.

Two days after scene 3.

Danny is begging.

Danny: Can you spare some change please? Mate you got any change?

Enter Sadie who storms past Danny.

Danny: Sadie. Hey Sadie!

Sadie: What!

Danny: Aren't you coming to see me?

Sadie: Why?

Danny: Because you're my friend?

Sadie: Your friend? What kind of a friend takes advantage of another and insults their kindness?

Danny: I haven't insulted you.

Sadie: You threw away a sandwich and bad mouthed charity.

Danny: Yeah, because you're wasting your time and not getting paid.

Sadie: I told you it's:-

Danny: All part of the mission. Why are you doing this?

Sadie: I couldn't get a summer job.

Danny: What?

Sadie sits.

Sadie: I came home after uni, hoping to get work to last until September. I couldn't find anything, so I signed up for 'Soul Fest'. I wanted to do something that kept me occupied and hopefully make some friends.

Danny: But you found me?

Sadie: It's not a bad thing. I'm glad I've found you again.

Danny: But?

Sadie: I just wish you wouldn't make such horrid remarks.

Danny: I have a right to speak my mind.

Sadie: I know, but you don't think how it might affect others. If I told you what I did today you would only react.

Danny: Well what have you done?

Sadie: I can't say.

Danny: I won't kick off.

Sadie: Ok, well today I did some graffiti cleaning.

Danny snorts.

Sadie: Oi.

Danny: Oh God it gets worse.

Sadie: It costs the council £2000 to remove the stuff.

Danny: So what's next?

Sadie: Running a youth café, giving out fluids to clubbers this Saturday night.

Danny: You're going to be doing all that?

Sadie: Sure.

Danny: Well beware of Jay and Ste, they'll rob you if you're not careful.

Sadie: Who are they?

Danny: A couple of the regulars at the Salvation Army.

Sadie: Do you stay there most evenings?

Danny: Yeah.

Sadie: Are you there tonight?

Danny: Yeah, if I can get a bed.

Sadie: What time do you leave?

Danny: Soon.

Sadie: I'll let you go then.

Danny: Where are you off?

Sadie: I'm on the evening shift in the 'Soul Café'. You should come down sometime.

Danny: Yeah maybe.

Both rise.

Danny gathers his things.

Sadie: Hope you get your bed.

Danny: Me too.

Sadie: Right I'd better be going. See you soon.

Danny: Yeah see ya.

Sadie: Bye.

Sadie exits.

Danny: It's never going to happen.

Danny exits in the opposite direction.

Exeunt.

Scene 6

Six years previously.

Danny and Sadie are lying by the riverbank.

Sadie: Danny?

Danny: Mm?

Sadie: Why do you like coming here?

Danny: Dunno, its quiet I guess.

Sadie: Don't you like town?

Danny: No, it's too busy, people rushing about, screaming kids, stuffy shops. Who wants that?

Sadie: But what about McDonald's or HMV?

Danny: What about them?

Sadie: Don't you like those places?

Danny: Yeah if I'm hungry, or I want a new game.

Sadie: Me and my friends always go to McDonald's first, then New Look.

Danny: Yeah.

Sadie: Danny?

Danny: Yeah?

Sadie: Why have I never met your Mum?

Danny: What do you mean?

Sadie: Well you've met my family. Why can't I meet yours?

Danny: You can't.

Sadie: Why?

Danny: You just can't that's all!

Sadie: Sorry.

Danny: Why do you want to know so much about my Mum?

Sadie: I'm curious.

Danny: Well don't.

Sadie: You can tell me.

Danny: I can't.

Sadie: Danny.

Danny: You wouldn't understand.

Sadie: Understand what?

Danny: You come from a nice home, parents are still together…

Sadie: What's up?

Danny: Nothing.

Pause.

Danny rises.

Danny: I'll see you tomorrow.

Sadie: Danny.

Danny exits.

Exeunt.

Scene 7

A week later.

Danny is waiting.

Enter Sadie.

Sadie: Hi, sorry I'm late.

Danny: It's ok.

Sadie: Miss kept us in for talking a lot.

Danny: Sadie:-

Sadie: Then my friend just wouldn't shut up about this older boy she fancies.

Danny: I'm leaving.

Sadie: You're leaving?

Danny: My Mum she…

Sadie: Oh Danny I…I'm sorry.

Pause.

Danny: It was lung cancer.

Sadie: Oh…

Danny: I'll be moving away.

Sadie: Where too?

Danny: My Aunt's.

Sadie: When do you go?

Danny: After the funeral?

Sadie: Do you want me to come?

Danny: No, it's ok.

Sadie: I'll miss you.

Danny nods.

Danny: Yeah, me too.

Exeunt.

Scene 8

Present Day.

Danny has resumed begging.

Enter Sadie tired.

Danny: Sadie

Sadie: Hi Danny.

Danny: You look knackered.

Sadie: I am.

Danny: What you been doing?

Sadie: Allsorts. It's been the final day of Soul Fest.

Danny: Has it?

Sadie: Yeah we had a live band and barbeque.

Danny: What did you do?

Sadie: Served drinks, did some nail painting.

Danny: That's it?

Sadie: I spoke to other visitors as well.

Danny: Cool.

Pause.

Sadie: Can't believe this mission is over.

Danny: So what's next?

Sadie: I'll be volunteering on a children's holiday camp in August, then eventually head back to Liverpool.

Danny: Will you come to visit me in the mean time?

Sadie: Sure, I promise.

Danny: You have a beautiful smile.

Sadie: Thanks.

Danny: It was what I fell in love with.

Sadie: Oh stop.

Danny: I'm serious.

Sadie: We were only 13.

Danny: So, it lit up the room so much, I couldn't take my eyes off:-

Sadie: Danny?

Danny: Yeah?

Sadie: What happened after you left school?

Danny: Why do you want to know?

Sadie: I'm curious, I haven't seen you in six years and now here you are living on the streets.

Danny: I went to a new school and had a hard time. Got into the wrong crowd and started taking drugs. My aunt got angry so kicked me out, before I took my GCSE's. Been homeless since. How about you?

Sadie: I completed school with five A*, stayed on in the sixth form…now I'm at university.

Danny: You had anymore boyfriends?

Sadie: Yes, one in sixth form, which didn't work out.

Danny: Who?

Sadie: You wouldn't have known him, he only joined us in year 12.

Danny: Oh right.

Sadie: Anyway, I had another one whom I met during fresher's week, then dumped him because he cheated on me. Now here I am.

Danny: Here you are.

Sadie: To be honest, I still have feelings for you too, but…

Danny: But?

Sadie: I should get going.

Danny: Will I see you next week?

Sadie: Of course…well bye.

Danny: Bye.

Sadie exits.

Danny: I love you.

Exeunt.

Scene 9

One week later.

Danny is in his usual place.

Enter Sadie.

Danny: Sadie.

Sadie walks past.

Danny: Hey Sadie!

Sadie: Oh hi Danny. Sorry I didn't see you there.

Danny: So how are you?

Sadie: I'm fine thanks. Sorry Danny, I've got to dash.

Danny: Where are you going?

Sadie: To meet my new boyfriend.

Danny: But what about me?

Sadie: What about you?

Danny: You said you still had feelings for me.

Sadie: Oh come on Danny, do you honestly expect us to get back together?

Danny: No but…

Sadie: Look Danny, times have changed. I've moved on now. So should you.

Danny: What about Soul Fest?

Sadie: What about it?

Danny: You were so loving and caring.

Sadie: That's ended now, I'm back in reality.

Danny: You'll never know what reality is, until it hits you in the face.

Sadie: Leave me alone.

Danny: Sadie please.

Sadie: I've really got to be going now.

Danny: Hey come back here. Sadie. Sadie!

Sadie exits.

Danny is left crying.

Exeunt.

Nikki Woods

Leah

December 23rd 2014, 7am

When I wake up, I test my moving parts - toes wiggle, check; fingers bend, check; and, onwards and upwards, eyes blink, check. Of its own accord, my stomach rumbles. Maybe it's the emptiness that makes me feel dizzy. Holding onto my trolley, I pull myself upright and balance in a standing position. I found the trolley at the municipal dump, but it's in surprisingly good condition. It has a tartan cover, which keeps out the rain, and it wheels along just fine. All my things fit snugly inside and it's strong enough for me to lean on when my feet begin to wilt. It's of the type preferred by old ladies - push not pull - but I'm pleased with the trolley. I'm glad it's mine. It's ideal.

The library doesn't open until 9.00 so I've got time to kill. Sometimes I sit in the park. I like to watch the children on their way to school, little ones running and mothers chasing. Or I head into the city to watch the coming and going of early morning workers. Feeling the bitingly cold wind on my back, the warmer of the two options is more tempting and so I point my trolley in the direction of the bus station.

Settling into a shelter, I pretend to wait for a bus. Like the regular passengers, I look up and down the road at the oncoming traffic, up and down, up and down, expecting that the bus will turn up and muttering and moaning when it doesn't.

'There's never the right bus when you need it,' I sigh, hoping no one will realise that, for me, all buses are equally wrong.

In the sub-zero temperature, my sighs form smoky clouds that hang in the wintery air. I take a deep breath to fill my lungs and exhale with a fiery force. Then do it again, more ferociously this time. A young mother walking past pulls her child close, protecting the little boy from the raging dragon. I smile and wave to show that I'm a not really monster, but just a girl. The mother only pulls her child closer.

December 31st 1999

Steve Marshall and Mya Vernon drive through streets swarming with party goers, all awaiting the magical moment the country's clocks will tick them into the 21st century.

'We're the only idiots working tonight,' Steve complains, but Mya knows that his gruff manner is merely a cloak for his anxiety.

As they drive north out of the city and cross the flyover, the Radley Estate looms above them. High rises that are the city's sink estate; Mya has never understood the language. They are heading to flat 802, which is located on the top floor of block D. It is the building used to house the city's most difficult families, or, as Mya prefers to think of them, the families most in need of support. Like Shona Jones and her daughter, who have been under Mya's supervision since the day Leah was born.

The emergency call out hadn't given them much to go on, just a vague message from a concerned neighbour about the continuous cries of a child. Cries that must have been loud enough to pierce a dividing wall, Mya reasons, as the familiar feelings of apprehension and dread churn in her stomach.

'Let's just hope the lift's in order.' Steve grimaces as he makes sure to lock up the car.

It takes them five minutes to climb the stairs and find the flat. Picking their way through the rubbish strewn hall and into the living room, the smell hits them sharp and strong. The mother is slumped on the sofa, her head hanging like a rag doll. The scene shows a history of self-harm escalated to self-destruction. The stench tells that the final annihilation was not recent.

'Leah!' The name of the child explodes in the room before Mya realises she is shrieking. 'Leah, where are you? It's okay, Leah. I'm here. Mya's here. It's all okay. Where are you?' The calls are met with silence.

'Over here,' Steve shouts, as he finds a padlock fixed to the outside of the bathroom door. Stunned at the thought of the horror that may wait inside, he looks at Mya. She makes no sound but nods her agreement. Steve breaks down the door.

At first they see nothing but, as their eyes become accustomed to the blackness, the heart-breaking image is exposed. A ragged blanket draped over the rim of the bath on one side and the toilet seat on the other. Underneath crouches Leah. The evidence of her recent tears is revealed in dried rivulets that run down her filthy face. But she is silent now and sits stone like, petrified in her makeshift home. The child wears a thin cotton nighty on which a portrait of the Little Mermaid has once appeared. Tears sting Mya's eyes as she sees that a small sprinkling of green sequins remains steadfastly in place.

December 23rd 2014, 10am.

'If you're happy and you know it, clap your hands. If you're happy and you know it clap your hands.' The children clap along and I do too, though I'm not allowed to take up room on the bright mats or cheerful chairs. I don't mind. I'm happy sitting behind the bookshelf where I can hear all the songs and stories. I'm hoping that my favourite will be read today. It's the tale of a tiger who comes to tea and eats everything in the house, leaving a little girl and her mum hungry. But the story has a happy ending when the dad comes home from work and they all go out for supper. I like to peep around the corner to see the picture of the family, all warm and cosy in the café.

Gilly wakes me up.

'Are you okay there?' She gently prods my arm. 'Leah, are you okay?'

The embarrassment which shows in my cheeks gives way to anxiety. Sleeping is not allowed in the library and I'm lucky that it's Gilly who's found me.

'I'm fine, I'm great,' I say, widening my eyes to appear alert.

'That's okay then, sweetie.' Gilly puts her hand on my shoulder. 'As long as you're okay.'

The truth is that I feel queasy and a bit sick, but I put on my coat and get ready to leave. In the warm security of the library, there's a danger I'll nod off again. I might not get away with it a second time.

August 1st 2001

Mya heaves the heavy box of files onto the table.

'Do they all relate to Leah Jones?' asks the Chair of the committee. Despite years of experience that enable him to view family tragedy as routine, he is disconcerted by the quantity of the accumulated documentation.

Mya starts with reports on Leah's medical history, consulting a tome of papers that detail everything from the consequences of her mother's Heroine use during pregnancy, to recent psychological assessments that report on the possibility of Reactive Attachment Disorder. The diagnosis is unsurprising in the light of the child's early emotional deprivation, but Mya is not wholly convinced. The dearth of foster carers makes it tempting to find fault with the child when things go wrong. And for Leah Jones, things have gone very wrong from the outset. Mya reads to the committee from a summary report:

> *Following the death of her mother, and a short period in an emergency foster placement, Leah Jones was taken into more permanent care on the 15th February 2000. Despite the experienced and knowledgeable home into which Leah was placed, she was unable to settle. Her*

violent outbursts, intentional urinating and uncontrollable screaming through the night led to the breakdown of the placement.

'Which shows how important it is for Leah to be provided with a home that offers security, stability and continuity.' The Chair of the committee takes refuge in the use of accepted jargon.

No one can take issue with that, thinks Mya, but she is worried about the conclusion that may be drawn.

'The wrong decision today would be worse that no placement.' Mya seeks to persuade the panel. 'Every failure in foster care undermines children's confidence, making the next placement less likely to succeed.'

Privately, recognising the truth of her own words, Mya worries that Leah may already be caught in the vicious cycle of rejection and abandonment.

December 23rd 2014, 4pm

She must have seen the reflection of my face in the charity shop window.

'Leah!' calls the voice that still makes me shudder. Feeling her close behind, I hunch my shoulders and bury my chin into my chest. But too late.

'Leah! Look, it's Leah from our old school.' A gang of girls crowd around.

'Leah, Leah, I wouldn't wanna be ya,' the voice shrieks and the gang burst into hysterical laughter.

They poke at me and someone pulls my hair. I'm taken back to Halthorpe High and the dread of each school day, not knowing what was in store. Mainly it turned out to be relentless taunts - my dirty clothes, ugly face or greasy hair. Sometimes it was worse – the strike of fear when word went out that one of the pack was 'after me' as terrifying as the later bullying blows. But now, as then, my tormentors soon get bored. I'm not worth much of their time.

'Wouldn't wanna be ya, wouldn't wanna be ya.'

Their spiteful chorus fades and I hear their boos and hisses trail away. Looking up, I watch them leave, arm in arm, with their boutique bags thrown carelessly over their shoulders.

When I'm sure they've gone and are not coming back, I push open the door to *CARE* and reverse myself and my trolley into the shop. The familiar smell cheers me up. It's something on which I can depend. I'm allowed to look around as long as I'm careful and don't get in anyone's way. I especially like the knick-knacks and, on my birthday, Linda gave me a little china rabbit. Apart from that, the ladies who volunteer are not allowed to offer me things - no blankets, shoes or clothes. It's like Linda says, if they gave away stuff to every homeless person who came through the door, they'd have no stock left. It's a shame because I could do with a new pair of trousers. The ones I've got on are cutting into me. I'm not sure why, I don't eat much. But if Linda's on duty and she often is, I can sit down for a chat and she'll sometimes make us a cup of tea. She's a good friend.

August 1st 2014

Steve Marshall pays for two large glasses of red wine.

'Cheers,' says Mya. 'Good to see you.'

It is the first time the two have been together since Steve retired. They've promised each other not to talk shop but, with the Statutory Review Meeting due to take place the following morning, Leah Jones is a natural topic of conversation. They have often relived the millennium eve call to the Radley Estate and have shared years of worry about Leah's progress in the care system.

'The problem is that she's never stayed anywhere long enough to develop a sense of belonging.' Mya sips at her wine, relieved to be with her reliable confidante. 'There's been one placement after another and no chance for her to develop a sense of her value and self-worth.'

Steve see's the frustration in Mya's face as she mulls over Leah's history.

'Now we're at the formal point of transition for a young woman who has no real sense of her own identity. I feel we've let her down. The system's definitely let her down.'

'But it's not your fault,' Steve says. A truth they both accept but know is not the point.

December 23rd 2014, 8pm

It's getting late and soon I'll need to decide where to sleep. I know where I ought to go – the same place I should have been for the last week - but I can't go back. I won't go back. It would have been alright if he hadn't arrived. The others in the house were nice, and I got along well with Julie, my new mentor. Like me, she loved stories and so we went to the library together. If Gilly saw us, she'd come over and the three of us would have a chat, just as ordinary people do. Mya had found me the place – a proper house in a proper street that I'd share with others. I was learning how to cook and we'd all chip in to keep the house clean and tidy. I was making friends. So it might have been okay, if it wasn't for him. If only he hadn't arrived. It's because of him that I can't go back. I won't go back.

Instead, I walk the streets, gazing up at the illuminated decorations which hang across the precinct: angels blow trumpets, Santas carry sacks and snowmen smile. *'Tis the Season to be Jolly'* broadcasts a banner strung between the bank and the pawn broker. 'Fa la la la la, la la la la,' I hum, as the snow begins to fall.

My trolley gets more difficult to push in the icy slush, but I keep walking. The city centre soon gives way to residential streets of neatly arranged houses. Peering inside, I see mothers cooking, children playing and families gathered around the TV. The windows of the homes reflect amber squares of cosiness and contentment onto the snow-covered pavement. Huddling inside my coat, I turn into the road that leads under the flyover and the high rises of the Radley Estate come into view. I've been told that I lived there once, when I was a little girl. When I was a girl who had a mother.

December 24th 2014, 7am

Toes wiggle, check. Fingers bend, check. Eyes blink, check. My stomach is tender and if I had a mirror to see my face, I'm sure it would look green. My body heaves and I'm sick in the porch of the church. Ashamed, I try to clear the mess, but the floor of the entrance is slippery and I trip against the door. It shifts and I fall, clutching at my trolley.

Inside, all is still and quiet. A light shines brightly and I follow it, walking up the long aisle towards the altar. It is there that I see baby Jesus. Below a star and in a stable, he slumbers peacefully under the ever watchful eye of his mother, Mary. The faithful shepherds gather round and the Kings bring their gifts. Joseph stands close by, the devoted father. On tip toe, I approach the familiar scene and, wrapping him in his muslin blanket, take Jesus from the manger. I hold him for a while, gently rocking the baby in my arms. I'd like to take him away with me, but know that he must be returned to where he is safe and sound. Pushing my trolley away from the light, I don't look back as I walk down the aisle, out of the church and into the cold.

August 1st 2015

Mya Vernon is working at her desk when the call comes through. She grabs her coat and bag and rushes from the office. The traffic is slow and it is over an hour before she pulls into the hospital car park. Navigating her way through a maze of corridors, Mya finally finds the ward. At the entrance she pauses, taking in the predictable scene – a team of professionals gather around a bed, speaking in hushed tones and concurring in nods and whispers. In the midst of the group is Leah Jones. Dressed in a hospital gown, she looks as vulnerable as the day Mya first found her. A little girl lost and alone in the world. In her arms, Leah holds her new born baby. She presses her lips softly to his head and cradles him with the warmth and tenderness of a mother's love.

Bethany Wilson

My Invisibility Cloak

I dreamed of being a superhero,
With powers beyond my dreams.
But now that I am invisible,
It's not quite as fun as it seems.

Tamsin Pearce

One Direction

Mummy says everything is going to be ok… and that I shouldn't worry about a thing. I'm not so sure… She had 'that look' on her face when she said it. The same 'look' she had when she told me my cat was going to get better… Milo died the next day. Mummy also said that 'It will be just like when we went to Bournemouth last summer and stayed at the bed and breakfast.' But I'm not stupid and I overheard her talking to Granny on the phone last night. Something about 'It's poky mum and on the wrong side of town?'

Funny isn't how your parents think you can't cope with really grown up stuff. Thing is, I was talking to my friend Lisa about things, at school yesterday, and her parents are divorced. She said that when her mum kicked her dad out, that things changed straight away, and that her mum even dyed her hair pink for a while! My mum and dad aren't getting divorced - they never even got married. Daddy always said they didn't have the time for it. Mummy said they couldn't afford it. So when he left last week, there was a lot of shouting and Mummy got really upset… she even threw his clothes out of the window. A couple of days later there was a 'For Sale' sign outside our home.

I asked Mummy why are we moving? She sat me down and said 'The Bank' were repossessing the house. I didn't really understand what she meant but she was already crying, so I just gave her a cuddle and stroked her hair. She then told me about us 'packing up our most special things', because we were going to be moving to a place called 'Redlands' for a few weeks. I asked her if could take my 'One Direction' poster with me. She said she thought that would be fine. But she did say I would have to think very carefully about anything else. She said we both would be sharing a room, so there wouldn't be much space, just 'cosy' I think was her word for it.

'Redlands' from the outside looks quite cool – it's a big house, with a red door and friendly face to it. But inside… it's horrible. We've got a room with a bathroom and if you look out the window you can see another brick wall – mum says it's the Pub next door. The room is quite small too. We haven't brought much with us and can hide it under the beds. Mum and I sleep next to each other and she is keeping a pint of milk in the sink, so I can have 'Shreddies' before I go to school in the morning…

It's really hot and stuffy too, the window is jammed half shut and the heating is stuck on, full blast. Mum says it will be ok and we are only here for a little while, so to try and make 'the best of a bad job'. But she has started smoking again. She has to balance on the bath edge and stick her hand out through the gap. I'm never going to smoke, it's just crazy and the smell makes me feel sick.... But she says it helps her 'relax' and as soon as we are 'sorted' she will give up. I've put my poster up on the wall at the end of the bed. I look at 'the boys' just before I go to sleep and first thing when I wake up – they look so happy... So innocent...

I was late for school today... I am never late for school. At our old house, I could lie in bed 'til seven thirty and still get to school for eight. But I can't sleep properly here and I didn't hear the alarm this morning. We have to leave by seven fifteen to catch a bus, Mummy goes with me. My school is on 'the other side' of town and she doesn't want me travelling on my own around here. It feels a bit scary and there was some bloke hanging around at the bus stop today. She says all this is only temporary and we are on 'the list'.

Lisa was really kind today. Her mum says I can go and stay at their's 'anytime I want'. But I don't want to leave mum at the moment. There was a load of noise last night at the B & B. It sounded like a fight. Mum said it was coming from outside the Pub but then later on, there was a shit load of banging and shouting in the room above us... I was really scared and mum and I pushed the chest of drawers up to the door. She stroked my hair and sang to me to try and get me to sleep. It didn't work. So I held her hand and looked at 'the boys'. They are so dreamy and gorgeous. They look so perfect... and smiley. I bet they've never had to live somewhere like this. It's a shithole.

Mum was on her mobile this afternoon after school and starting screaming and shouting at someone. I've never heard her so angry. She went into the bathroom for a smoke and I heard her saying 'No way, no fucking way. We cannot live like this any longer.... I'm close to a nervous fucking breakdown... You have to find us somewhere else.' She talked about someone called 'Charlie' I think... And said that the people down stairs were taking him somewhere? I only caught half of the conversation. I put my music on to try and drown it out. Lisa has lent me her iPod whilst I'm here... Now I can listen to 'the boys' all day, everyday... I've found heaven on earth! I love 'You and I' – It feels like they wrote it just for me.

I am covered in bites... They really hurt and I'm off school. Mum got me some cream to stop them itching and I keep having a shower to try and stop me scratching them.., Mum has taken some photos and says it will help us with 'the list'. She tried to explain, something about a 'points' system, and how the more we get, the quicker we get somewhere else to live? I don't really understand how points can help us. All I know is it feels like we are both doing a prison sentence at the moment. Mum has started drinking Gin just before she goes to bed now. She calls it her 'night cap' but I caught her having one this morning before we left for school and I could smell it on her, on the bus...

I saw Dad at the weekend. He looked really tired. Says he has a small bedsit he is renting, just whilst he gets straight. He and mum didn't speak. They both looked very angry with each other when he picked me up. He took me to KFC for lunch, as a treat he said, but I told him we live off takeaways at the moment, unless we go to Grans or a friends for tea, so it would be really good to go back to his. He said 'not this time love', 'just need to get it right before you see it', but I knew he was lying. I think where he is staying is even worse than our's. Maybe he needs to collect 'points' too, before he moves? He says work is being great and have even given him a couple more shifts. And I saw him give mum some cash when he dropped me off.

At school its getting really embarrassing. I can't wait for the summer holidays. I don't want anyone, apart from Lisa, to know we are homeless. And my uniform is starting to smell now. Mum washes my clothes in the sink at the B and B, and we do go to the Laundrette sometimes, but everything comes out smelling scorched and of wee. I think it's the dryers or something. Mum won't leave me there on my own. It's where a lot of kids, older ones, hang out. And when you wait outside you can smell their spliffs. They hang around in groups. I will never smoke or drink or take drugs... We've just done all about it at school.

Mum met me from school today. She never does that. She was in a cab. She never takes a cab. She said she had just been to the Council, again, and that we had moved up the list. Apparently there's a flat which we might be able to have. So on the way back to the B & B, we went to check it out from the front. It looks a bit grim, a high rise, but as mum says, it will be close to school and Lisa only lives about five minutes away. I know she is disappointed but after two months now of living here, it's going to feel like a palace. And I can have my own room again. Mum says it's only got one bedroom but she will sleep in the front room. I can't wait.

I got mugged today, on the way home from the corner shop. I was listening to the iPod and this boy ran by me and grabbed it. He caught my face with his cigarette. Mum has put some cream on it and says she will talk to Lisa's mum, try and do a deal, pay her back monthly or something. It happened so quick I didn't really have time to be scared but now I am just bloody mad. I am starting to feel like we can't go any further down, mum and I. It's not fair. Adults always bang on about 'childhood, being the happiest time of your life' but my childhood stopped the minute Dad left. This is shit and I can't see a way out. Even 'One Direction' can't help anymore. They just look like fakes – polished, air brushed and unreal. This is real and I don't want it.

We got it! We got the frigging flat and are moving over there tonight after school. I can't believe it, it's amazing. Mum says it's only temporary but I don't care either way. It's a new start and I've told her not to worry and that things can only get better for us. She is smiling but her eyes still show her worry. Seems like the mugging was a blessing in disguise; we finally got enough 'points' to get moved. I can't help thinking about what it's like for other people in our situation. Especially children. 'Home is where the heart is', so they bang on about, but when your home is a shit heap, small and frightening, the strongest heart can't fix that, can it?

I'm leaving 'the boys' on the wall here, for the next people that move in. They have been keeping me going whilst we've been here and deep down I do still fancy them, especially Liam, who is gorgeous. I still like their music too, although now I'm nearly 12, I guess I am getting a bit too old for boy bands! Lisa has gone off them too, she likes Collaboro. She reckons that they are more mature, well they are in their 20s! I think 'One Direction' probably smoke dope, get pissed and have lots of sex when the cameras aren't on them. Maybe they do, maybe they don't. But I've got my eye on a boy at school now, called Chris. He is just lovely and lives about ten minutes away from our new home. He isn't a musician but he does like chips and football.

Mums got a 'start up loan' for the flat. She's almost getting excited about it now. It's enough to cover a sofa bed for her and a bed for me. She says when she can find a job, we can splash out on anything else we want. I don't really care about 'stuff' anymore. I used to. Thought it was important to have all the latest gadgets, phones and clothes. The house was full of things, most unpaid for, turns out. Maybe Mum and Dad tried to hide their unhappiness with each other by buying lots of things to compensate? Turning into a right psychoanalyst I am. Maybe I'm just growing up. Whatever, just can't wait to get settled, have my own room and feel safe again. I'm going to look after mum from now on and the only way for us two is up!

Jane Anne Rogers

The Princess Mary Tin

"Now then," the old man said.

Johnny pulled his cap down to hide his face but he knew he'd been seen.

The dead end ginnel behind the canal bridge was all his and he didn't want anyone sticking their nose in.

A fortnight back it had saved him from the rain. His only thought on the twelve mile stretch from his Ma's was where to sleep. He'd ended up here. Dodging out of the rain he'd found just enough room for a scraggy lad, a rucksack and a blanket.

He'd been glad it was wet. Tramping out of Keighley he could pretend the tears were just raindrops.

That moment, when he found the ginnel… and realised that he didn't have to go back… it was the best of his life.

The lads at the mill thought he was rooming at his auntie's in town.

He let them think it.

He could walk to the chippie with them, share a Woodbine and a laugh and then stroll off down the towpath.

Home.

It wasn't what most folks would call home. There was no fireside, no furniture…and no Ma. But he felt safe here.

There was nobody breathing down his neck; waiting for him to say or do the wrong thing. He could lean back against the stone wall and peer at the back of the mill through the hawthorn knowing that no-one was after him.

No more bruised ribs or black eyes. It was dry, it was sheltered and it was peaceful. He could rest here.

The place smelt of happier times, of cow parsley and pipe smoke and old jokes. Sixty or seventy years back, the navvies who built the canal had sat here. He imagined them, aching and sweaty, swapping mugs of milky tea and stories of families far away.

Ma would be proud; he'd tidied up nicely. He'd put newspaper on the earth floor and he'd rigged up a bit of twine to sling wet laundry on. There was a loose brick behind some bracken where he hid his keepsakes.

There wasn't much.

A copy of *White Fang*, his Ma's hanky and the Princess Mary Tin.

And now this had happened.

He snuffed out the flame but the old chap had definitely spotted him.

"I see thee," the voice said again. "What's goin' on down there? If you're up to no good now's the time to stop."

Johnny struggled out through the undergrowth.

He held out his arms, palms forward as if to prove his innocence. "Nothing goin' on Mister. Just restin'."

"Thought so." The man said. "So… for three week since…maybe more…you've been there, 'ave you?" He paused and then repeated Johnny's own phrase sarcastically. "Restin'?"

"How d'you know that?" asked Johnny.

"Nipper 'ere, he let me in on it," he looked down at the Jack Russell by his feet. "Didn't thee lad?"

The dog wagged its stumpy tail enthusiastically.

The man turned back to Johnny, more certain now. "Well you're not what I expected, I'll tell thee that."

Johnny frowned. "What d'you mean?"

The way the man was with the dog had calmed him a little. Maybe he could talk his way out of trouble?

"I thought p'raps Nipper 'ad found a gang o' pirates or 'alf a dozen fancy women at least!" said the man. "Not a scrap of a lad barely out of short trousers." He held out his hand. "Edwin Spencer… Spence, if you will."

Johnny grasped the hand and came out from the shadow. The violet dusk over the canal threw a strange light over them as if they had stepped onto a stage. For a moment they were uncertain what to do. It was Spence who took the initiative.

"Well Nipper and me 'ave another 'alf mile of towpath to do. That's our regular evenin' wander, eh Nip?" The dog seemed to agree and Spence turned back to Johnny.

"So if you've nowt better on, will you take a turn with us?"

The good thing about Spence, Johnny discovered, was that he didn't ask too many questions.

Sometimes his pals at work were just too curious.

And they wanted things from him. Things he couldn't give, like his company at the pictures or the game. He didn't want to get close to them. He wasn't going to tell them about his Ma, or about Joe.

Their casual grumbles showed him that there were people in their lives that cared.

People who darned their socks, or made a good shepherd's pie or were just there when they got home. None of them would be able to understand why he'd needed to come up the dale for work. And none of them knew that he was sleeping behind the canal arch.

"You were lucky then, getting' a job there, they've not been tekin' any on lately." Spence said.

"Aye," said Johnny. "Timin' was spot on. The foreman 'ad just 'ad a set-to with a sweeper-upper. I said I'd done it afore and that was that."

"You're a grand 'un," said Spence. "It's a tough ol' place."

"Too 'ot and too noisy," said Johnny. "I know that much. But I get on alright. An' I get fifteen shillin' for it."

Spence had worked at the mill himself years back. He liked hearing about all the changes.

"Business was bad after the war," he said. "No more uniforms and tents."

Johnny kicked a stone into the canal. "War's jus' bad all round," he said.

Johnny got into the habit of walking down to meet them on the canal path. Sometimes he'd save a few scraps of batter for Nipper. The little Jack Russell would jump up at him happy and yelping.

"'The boy's spoilin' thee lad," Spence told the dog, but Johnny knew he was pleased.

There were one or two others he was getting to know too. A woman with a big black pram and a couple of little ones would smile and nod at him in between scolding 'our Billy'.

There was a youngish chap with a whippet. He would pass them apologetically whilst Spence held on to Nipper, wriggling and growling.

No-one else knew where he slept though.

Two or three weeks after they met Johnny took the Princess Mary Tin from his pocket and showed it to Spence.

"Whose is this then?" the old man asked.

He turned the tin over in his hand, his craggy joints a sharp contrast to the smooth shine of the brass. The engraved profile of the Princess stood youthful against the old white flesh of his thumb. 'Christmas 1914' shone out bravely.

"Yours?" said Spence.

Johnny nodded, swallowing hard. He could almost smell the nutmeg from the kitchen dresser he'd taken the tin from.

"I brought it with me, from Ma's."

Spence opened the tin, it was empty.

"It was me dad's," said Johnny.

He coughed loudly to stop himself from crying. He didn't want Spence thinking he was soft.

"Ma wanted me to 'ave it. It 'ad tobacco in," he said.
"It's in good nick. It's eight years ago or more now. All the men servin' that Christmas got one like this," said Spence.
"Me mum tried to keep me a few bits… y'know of dad's… she's looked after it."
Spence ran a thumb round the empty tin. "Did your dad smoke the tobacco before …" His voice trailed away.
Johnny shook his head. "No. No, 'e didn't."
He paused before continuing. "Me step-dad, Joe," he said. His jaw set determinedly as he thought about it. "'E likes 'is ale."
Spence looked down at the tin, "And?"
"I s'pose 'e was fed up with me. Wanted to get at me. So 'e took the baccy." Johnny said. "Me Ma said I should have it. Twenty-first birthday; celebrate with a roll-up. She reckon'd me dad would've wanted me to think of 'im then. Said 'e'd be proud of me."
Spence stopped turning the tin in his hand and met Johnny's eye,
He put his hand on the boy's shoulder for moment. "Tough for you son. Tough. An' I'm guessin'," he said, "That your step-dad… it wasn' jus' that 'e took the tobacco?"
Johnny bit his lip. "'E's vicious. Y'know, 'e's rough when 'e's 'ad a few. He takes 'is belt to me. Goes for me Ma too. She's allus cryin'. I can't stop 'im." His chin wobbled and he looked away from Spence and towards the canal.
"'E frightens you does 'e lad?" Spence asked.
"It's not jus' that," said Johnny. "It's like 'e…" He paused for a moment thinking, "me step-dad… 'e makes me feel like I don't matter'," he shook his head, "like I'm nowt."
Spence spat towards the grasses by the path as if trying to get rid of a bad taste.
"So it's better livin' down there? Campin' out?" Spence asked, nodding towards at the canal arch.
Johnny shrugged, "S'pose. It's better than bein' at 'ome anyway."
"An' this Joe's an ol' soldier too is 'e?" said Spence.
"Yeah. Me dad's pal. They were in the West Ridin' together."
"Well lad, soldier or no, that's no way to treat anyone. An' you don't need that."
"I know," said Johnny, taking the tin back and rubbing its shine along his sleeve. "That's why I left."

The next night it was raining but Johnny finished his chips and scrambled out of the ginnel when he heard Spence's footstep.
But it wasn't Spence.

"So this is it? Tunnelling away like a rat are ya?" Joe grabbed his shirt and wrapped it around his hand so that the boy was straight-jacketed and yanked towards him.

"My mate said 'e'd seen ya….damned right 'e was too! I said straight off…that'll be just like that sneaky bugger! Dirty little sod! Livin' out like a bloody stray dog!"

He was so close that it was impossible for Johnny to look anywhere but into his face. The yellowing teeth, the unshaven chin with a trail of spit all reminders of the horrors of his Ma's house. He tried to meet the older man's eyes without blinking.

He didn't want Joe to see how terrified he was. He mustn't cry. He could see everything slipping away from him. The job at the mill, his walks with Spence….Joe was going to knock it all aside. He'd be nowt again.

The twisted jacket made him stoop forwards; he tried to straighten. "You can't make me go back!" he yelled.

"Ohhh!" said Joe leering. He laced his fingers through Johnny's hair and jerked the boy's head backwards. "Can't I? Somethin' special 'bout you is there? An' do the local coppers know you're living 'ere?"

Joe's fingers dug deep into his collar bruising his skin and lifting him from the ground. The smell of Joe, the beer on his breath was threatening to drown him.

"An' your poor bloody mother…does she deserve…." started Joe and then yelped in pain and surprise.

"Ahh! Damn an' blast….soddin' dog!" he said. He kicked out in anger and then shook his leg cursing and trying to loosen Nipper's grip on his ankle.

"Off Nipper!" said Spence. "And you!" he shouted at Joe, "Leave that boy be!"

More in shock than anything else Joe let Johnny go.

"An' who are you?" he asked. "This is my lad. 'E's comin' 'ome to me an' 'is mother."

"Doesn't look like 'e wants to go! I s'pose this is the way you plan to treat 'im is it?"

Johnny opened his mouth to protest but Spence beat him to it. "You're not tekin' 'im! No chance!" he said. "I'm not 'avin' it! I'll not allow you to tek 'im."

"Listen ol' man," Joe leaned in fist clenched. "I've seen off braver men than you…I've no bayonet with me, but I'll stop you all the same."

Nipper growled and Joe drew back. With one eye on the dog he continued, his voice changed, whining in an attempt to persuade. "See sense now," he said. "The boy's 'ome is with 'is mother. You know I can't leave 'im sleepin' on the canal bank!"

Johnny pulled himself upright. "My mother! Don't you dare say anythin' about her! Or me! What do you care about me!" He pulled up his shirt. "Look? See anythin'?"

Both men were silent. Johnny slapped the palm of his hand against the flat of his bare stomach.

"No!" he said triumphantly. "You can't see nothin'! Not even a bruise! Cos' I've not 'ad one kickin' in weeks! An' you want me to go back to that!"

Joe shook his head slowly, unwilling to listen. He tried Spence again. "You can see what 'e's like! The boy's a proper 'andful! I don't want 'im gettin' into more bother."

"No need for that," said Spence. "If 'e wants 'e can come 'ome with me," he looked across at Johnny. "If he wants to?"

Johnny nodded, eyes shining with tears. He couldn't speak.

Joe wiped the back of his hand across his mouth clumsily like someone waking from a deep sleep. For a moment he was still and then he turned to the boy.

"You're a disgrace," he said. "No backbone! Good job your country isn't relyin' on the likes of you….If we'd all been like you…" he looked around wildly, "the Kaiser'd be 'ere now!"

Spence stepped forward and grabbed Joe's arm.

"It's no excuse y'know…that ol' 'King and country' routine. Yes, you'll 'ave suffered. Yes, you'll 'ave lost your pals…an' maybe the ale 'll soften some of that. But this lad…an' 'is mother come to that…they don't deserve a pummelin' just cos you feel sorry for y'sen."

"And what d'you know ol' man! What d'you know 'bout me?" He bared his teeth and if it wasn't for the dog Johnny was sure that he would have swung for Spence.

Spence smiled and stepped back, his grey eyes shining. He raised his hands as if giving a simple explanation.

"Because of me own lad. Saw 'im when he was 'ome on leave. I 'eard 'im scream out in 'is sleep. Saw 'im jump when the kitchen fire crackled….I watched 'im slam 'is fist into a doorframe…jus' to feel summat."

Joe looked down at the towpath. His shoulders stooped. Suddenly he looked shorter, older.

He turned back to Spence. "You take 'im then. An' good riddance."

He walked away but then after a few paces he slowed.

"Did he come back…your boy?" he said.

Spence shook his head. "No," he said. "Lost. Verdun."

Joe nodded. "Maybe 'e was lucky," he said. Then he gestured towards Johnny. "You maybe won't believe me sayin' this...but, tek care of him."

They watched as he stumbled off down the towpath. It wasn't clear if it was the shock of the old man's words or the beer which was making him stagger and in truth Johnny didn't care.

He was free.

He turned to Spence.

"Did you mean it? You know, when you said I could stay at yours?"

Spence smiled. "Course I did. There's jus' me an' Nipper an' our manners is rough. Ain't they Nip?"

"I'll bring my wage in....I'll not be in the way..."

Spence raised his hand. "You'll need to work lad; I've no brass. But we shall be glad to 'ave you."

"An' are you sure...is there room for me?" Johnny asked.

Spence bit his lip and bowed his head and for a moment. Johnny thought the old man might cry.

"There's my boy's ol' room. There's a bed, an' a chair....an' a bit of a shelf...." He paused and then continued, only the tiniest of breaks in his voice. "That shelf already 'as one Princess Mary tin on it...but I there's room for yours too. We'll keep their memory together."

Johnny didn't trust himself to speak.

And when Spence spoke it wasn't to Johnny but to the Jack Russell sitting next to them on the canal bank.

"Come on then Nip! Lead the way! Let's get this lad home!"

Char March

They just use dogs to get more dosh

– it shouldn't be allowed *

This is my person
He sleeps beside me

I have had him for two years
I found him in a Waitrose car park

I brought him some newspapers
My person likes newspapers – and cardboard

He gave me a cream cake from the bin
He tied himself to me with this string

This is our home
It glitters with smells

It is best in winter
Then the metal tubes blow hot air

In summer it is cars' barks
And there are loud people

They come and kick my person
They try to kick me

Sometimes he is sick
I usually eat his sick

Then I take him to the big place that echoes
They give him a hot bowl

They give me crunchy bits and a stroke
Then they scare my person with pieces of paper

He takes his cardboard
He takes my blanket

I lead him back home

**Heard on a BBC Radio Leeds phone-in about people sleeping rough in the city.*

Carmel Page

Two Cushions and a Pillow

When you click on the UK Immigration Office's website the first thing you see is a pair of handcuffs.

The website explains that you should claim asylum when you first enter the country. Once in the country the only place where you can claim asylum is Immigration House in Croydon. The website says that when you go to Croydon you must take with you four unseparated passport-style photographs with your name and date of birth written on the back of each photograph. This is complete rubbish. When you go to claim asylum what you must take is a cushion.

On arrival at Immigration House you hand over your identity documents. They tell you to stand by the wall and look at the camera. They take your photograph. They don't tell you not to smile; you won't be smiling. They tell you to place the first finger of your right hand on a small plastic block. Now they have your finger print. They examine your paperwork. They decide who you are. They decide on your date of birth. They accompany you upstairs in a lift and they decide on which floor you can get out.

As you leave the lift security officers ask you your name. They look at you then they look at the photograph of you on their computer screen, they look back at you. They check your fingerprint. They have to be sure you have not switched your identity whilst being accompanied upstairs in the lift. They escort you through a locked door. They tell you to sit and wait. The seating is two metal bars like the seating in a bus shelter. There is no bus coming. There is no shelter. You will wish you had brought a cushion.

*

Maimoona Mesiyah does not claim asylum when she first enters the country, she has been warned not to. She has paid her agent to claim asylum on her behalf and to sort out all of her legal documents for her. She knows that once she has the correct legal documents she cannot be sent back.

The Immigration officer checks Maimoona's visa.

"Tankyou," she says, it's one of her few English words. She thinks they must be able to see her heart pounding beneath her shalwar kameez but they let her in. England. Safety. A man walks straight up to her.

"Maimoona Mesiyah?" He is smiling and friendly, it catches her off guard, she is expecting the agent here to be more furtive, whispering to her to follow him at a distance as they had done before. She is also expecting him to use the name on her passport whilst they are still in the airport, not her real name. She is worried that this is a trick. "Welcome to England," he says in her native language. "You had a good journey? We will look after you and take you to your contact, I have arranged a place for you to stay tonight but first I must just take your passport for ten minutes. I will be straight back. Wait for me here and do not talk to anyone."

"Thank you." Maimoona says. She would rather wait somewhere quieter, she feels very exposed in the brightly lit airport but she knows it is just for ten minutes. She is imagining what she will say when she phones her parents, they will be amazed at how easily she has left one country and entered another. But not yet, she will call them when she is away from the airport and no one can hear.

Maimoona sees a yellow-haired woman run to an orange-haired man; even the man's arms have orange hair! She hears people talking in languages which sound like words said upside-down. Her scarf slides a little and she instinctively pulls it back across her forehead although there is clearly no need to do this here. She can see women with exposed hair and naked arms and legs and half of their chests who are walking about as if they think they are fully clothed. She glances at people to check if they are watching her but no one seems to be. She keeps telling herself her troubles are now thousands of miles away but she can't help thinking that if she can change countries so easily then the threat can follow her too. She waits for her agent to return. Her heartbeat slowly calms.

An hour passes. Maimoona realises she did not notice which direction the agent went in so she is looking every way, all of the time. Another hour passes, there are less people and there seem to be more security guards. She is worried that the security guards are watching her but she doesn't dare to look at them to see. After three hours she decides to sit on a chair, there are now so few people the agent is certain to spot her when he comes back. She wants the toilet but doesn't dare to go in case she misses him. After four hours the security men are definitely watching her. She does not know if they watch everyone who is waiting for a long time or if they have been informed about her.

After four and a half hours Maimoona draws her mobile out of her pocket as if it has gone off in silent mode.

"Hello." she says in her own language. She pauses. "Don't worry I am fine but I was concerned when you weren't here to meet me." Pause. "I'll make my own way there then. What is the best way to get there?" Pause. "Yes I think I can do that, I will see you soon." She picks up her small bag and walks off as confidently as she can. She finds the toilet then walks out into the night.

The air is cold but not dark, orange dark she thinks. Her clothing shivers. There are lots of signs and cars. She knows she has to get away from the airport. She sees another young woman wearing clothes like hers who looks, like her, to be late teens. Maimoona catches her eye and smiles. She mutters a prayer as she walks up to her.

"Hello," she says in the only language she knows, "I have just arrived here, I don't know anyone and I have no money, my agent took my passport over four hours ago and he has not come back, please, can you help me?"

Squashed into the back of a warm car Maimoona tries to see how this new world looks but as the wheels rotate her eyelids roll down over her eyes. They arrive at a smart house. The people she is with are welcomed warmly then they explain about her. They give her food but don't ask her any questions.

"You can stay tonight but you will have to sleep on the sofa."

"Thank you."

They give her a blanket and she rests her head on a cushion. There is a battle during the night. The need to stay alert and listen to every sound, assess every creak, every distant laugh, fights against the need to rest, recuperate, recharge before the next day. Sleep wins. Fear has its own tactics and ambushes her in the hours when all is so quiet she strains to hear anything at all.

Next day the young woman tells Maimoona to go with an older man in his car. The man in the car has the radio on loud, he does not talk to her and she does not understand what is said on the radio. She is very frightened because they are driving on the wrong side of the road and she thinks they will be hit. He parks on a road of red brick houses just like the ones in picture books of England. She is taken into the back of one of the houses. They do not stop to take their shoes off. They pass through a kitchen into a room full of boxes. The boxes all have a picture of a leaf on them, she knows what this particular leaf is; it is a bad omen.

A young man is sitting on one of the boxes smoking.

"This is the new one, put her with the other women," the driver says. The room smells as if the man has spent his whole life smoking there. He takes her upstairs, her nose tells her they are passing a toilet, then they enter a dark storeroom with deep shelves on each side. The man points at one of the lower shelves.

"Get some sleep now," he says, "you will be working tonight." The man goes.

Maimoona stands with one shoulder touching each shelf. She can now make out the rounded shapes of five people asleep. They have a shelf each like bunk beds but for three people. She feels the empty shelf, there is a mattress on it and a sheet, a folded blanket too. She wonders if the sheet is clean. She puts down her bag, takes off her shoes, bends down, crawls onto the mattress and lies down. She can tell that the sheet is not clean. The room is warm and airless, she reaches above her and can feel the bed above without even straightening her arms. She can hear men talking loudly nearby and boots on the stairs. She hugs the thin pillow and prays about the type of work she will be asked to do at night-time. Some hours later she is woken by the light being turned on.

Downstairs the oldest woman gives her square white food from a plastic bag. They use the word *bread* for it. It is not much like bread but it is good toasted. The women seem like normal women and they speak her language. She needs to know if they have normal jobs. What do they do? What will she have to do? She cannot ask, she cannot make the words move inside her mouth. One of the women jumps when she hears the back door open. She jumps at everything, but the other four seem quite calm. A man comes in and goes upstairs without speaking to them.

They all walk out of the house without stopping to change their footwear. It feels like walking out without saying goodbye. They pass a few houses and go down a passageway, then cross the road. Crossing the road confuses Maimoona because the cars are coming at her the wrong way. It doesn't help that she is shaking so much. She crosses when the other women cross. She looks up and down the road and wonders whether she should run away.

"Come on," the other women say. She senses they want to share something with her. Perhaps they want to share something good. Perhaps they want her to take a share of something bad to reduce the badness for them. The older woman takes her by the arm, Maimoona feels it would be disrespectful to pull away so she follows the women around the corner and they enter a building.

The building is like a warehouse and she can hear a thumping sound like a hammer, it is her own heart. There are men working there, they glance up at the women then carry on working. Maimoona is taken into a cramped office to a man called Saleem. There is a clear area on his desk where he puts his laptop and opens it. The clear area is like a bay surrounded by cliffs and landslides of paperwork. Saleem stares at her, he stares right into her eyes and does not look pleased. She sees a dark cloud of eyebrows and looks shyly away. He types something on his lap top.

"The girls will show you what to do," he says.

The women take Maimoona to a lorry behind the warehouse. It is full of boxes of heavy tins of paint which they unload and stack in a corner. Then Maimoona sees that the lorry is not full of paint, it is only a layer behind the doors. There are bigger but lighter boxes behind them which are bulky to carry. She thinks the reason that she cannot read the writing on the boxes is because she is crying so much. When her tears eventually stop she realises the reason she cannot read the writing is because it is in a foreign language. Once the lorry is unpacked they sort through the boxes, there are eight different types. The other women explain that they contain cigarettes from Russia and the local shops want some of each type. They repack them so that each box has the full selection in it. Then they have to load all the boxes into vans ready for delivery. The air is now cold each time they take the boxes outside to where the vans are parked in darkness. She pulls her scarf tightly around her. Maimoona startles every time the jumpy girl jumps and she can tell the girl is embarrassed about this. Maimoona feels as if she is the one at fault.

At midnight a man comes with food in square foil bowls with lids. Relief about the nature of the work almost overwhelms Maimoona but she makes herself focus on the food. The food is hot and good, they eat it in a side-room where there are some old chairs and a sofa which sinks around her when she sits on it. They go back to work packing sweets with smiley faces on them. She is told they are not sweets they are pills. She wonders if they are pills to make you happy, if they are she will eat them all.

At five in the morning they get more food. They finish work at eight. Saleem gives everyone money as they leave. Some of them get notes. Maimoona gets six thick round coins and some instructions.

"Do not talk to anyone you don't know. Do not go anywhere other than where these women take you. If you do I will call the Police. As long as you work for me you can live in my house. Go there now and get some sleep so that you can work tomorrow."

Leaving the building with the other women Maimoona is dazzled by the bright morning sunlight. They all stand at the side of the road watching for a gap in the traffic. She is still confused about which way to look first. The older woman links arms with her.

"Now," she says leading her across the road. "Let's get home to bed." Maimoona thinks of her family home. She wonders how long the woman must have lived on a shelf to be calling it her home. Back at the house they do not take their shoes off until they get to their room. She waits on the landing with the other younger ones, there is not room for them all to get undressed at once. She lies down on her mattress with her head on the thin pillow and thinks that the sheets are not clean. She is woken by the light being turned on.

The women have a little time when they wake to go to the local shops before work. They walk down a busy road and pass a green field behind a fence. Maimoona has always thought that England is where white people live amongst green fields and castles. The women tell her it is a school field and only the children can walk on it. They pass a building which has a sign outside with a picture of a castle and men on horses. They tell her it is a public drinking house. She sees a few white people but most of the locals are not white. The women tell her the white people live in a better area.

The women help Maimoona to buy credit for her phone. She calls her agent. Many times she calls her agent, in the evening when she wakes, in the morning before sleeping, whenever she awakes in the middle of the day from her recurring nightmare about not being able to escape from the men, she hugs her thin pillow and calls her agent. The call is never answered. She thinks they may be too busy claiming asylum for her and sorting her legal documents to have time to answer the phone.

Maimoona knows they are never going to answer the phone but her fingers remember the pattern of the number and she still keeps trying to contact them.

Maimoona knows that they are not sorting her legal documents. She knows that there will never be any legal documents.

She still keeps calling them.

Maimoona calls her parents many times too and they always answer. Even when she is confused about the time difference and they are in bed, they still always answer. Maimoona tells her parents that she has a good job in a factory making sweets with smiley faces. She tells them her boss is very kind to her. She tells them that she lives in a lovely home made of red bricks and she has many new friends. She tells them that the legal documents take a long time to be processed but she should have asylum soon. She tells them that she walks through green fields when she goes to the shops and she passes a castle with men on horses outside it. She tells them she is safe.

"Are you sure you are safe now?" her mother asks her.

"Yes," she assures her mother, "it is wonderful to be in England and I know I am safe."

Afterword

When my colleague Tina came to me with the idea that SASH should run a creative writing competition, I was instinctively cautious. In the scheme of things SASH is a tiny charity; albeit thanks to our volunteers, we 'punch above our weight'. Was it really appropriate to put our scarce resources into a project like this? What convinced me was the chance to raise awareness of homelessness and our brilliant solution to the problem, in such an innovative way; the possibility that Ross Raisin, whose writing I already admired, might be willing to help was a big plus too.

Looking back my fear was that our efforts would not be rewarded by either the quality or quantity of entries. My fear was misplaced; the quality of more than 120 entries ensured that our volunteer judges spent many hours deliberating before sending Ross our shortlist- the 22 pieces contained in this anthology.

We took pains to encourage entries from people with personal experience of homelessness and it was pleasing that some of our shortlisted entries were in this category. For me the authenticity of these entries shines through. Many pieces describe in telling detail the fear and isolation of vulnerable young people suddenly adrift in a frightening adult world. And this is where SASH comes in. Our volunteers help young people by giving up their spare-room, whether in an emergency or for the longer-term, so that we and our partners can provide the help and support they need to avoid the devastating effects of homelessness so graphically described throughout this anthology.

To pick up Ross's reflection on the word 'home' we do the best we can for our young people to meet as many of the meanings conveyed by that word; meanings that often only become fully apparent in its absence- 'homelessness'.

Our thanks to all who helped to organise this project and to all who submitted an entry.

Peter Robinson
Director
SASH

Other anthologies and collections available from Stairwell Books

First Tuesday in Wilton	Ed. Rose Drew and Alan Gillott
The Exhibitionists	Ed. Rose Drew and Alan Gillott
The Green Man Awakes	Ed. Rose Drew
Fosdyke and Me and Other Poems	John Gilham
frisson	Ed. Alan Gillott
Gringo on the Chickenbus	Tim Ellis
Running With Butterflies	John Walford
Late Flowering	Michael Hildred
Scenes from the Seedy Underbelly of Suburbia	Jackie Simmons
Pressed by Unseen Feet	Ed. Rose Drew and Alan Gillott
York in Poetry Artwork and Photographs	Ed. John Coopey and Sally Guthrie
Her House	Donna Marie Merritt
Taking the Long Way Home	Steve Nash
Chocolate Factory	Ed. Juliana Mensah and Rose Drew
Skydive	Andrew Brown
Still Life With Wine and Cheese	Ed. Rose Drew and Alan Gillott
Somewhere Else	Don Walls
Sometimes I Fly	Tim Goldthorpe
49	Paul Lingaard
Satires	Andy Humphrey
The Ordinariness of Parrots	Amina Alyal
New Crops from Old Fields	Ed. Oz Hardwick
Throwing Mother in the Skip	William Thirsk-Gaskill
The Problem With Beauty	Tanya Nightingale
Learning to Breathe	John Gilham

For further information please contact rose@stairwellbooks.com
www.stairwellbooks.co.uk
@stairwellbooks